Pedagogies for Building Cultures of Peace

International Issues in Adult Education

Series Editors

Peter Mayo (*University of Malta, Msida, Malta*)

Editorial Advisory Board

Stephen Brookfield (*University of St Thomas, Minnesota, USA*)
Waguida El Bakary (*American University in Cairo, Egypt*)
Budd L. Hall (*University of Victoria, BC, Canada*)
Astrid von Kotze (*University of Western Cape, South Africa*)
Alberto Melo (*University of the Algarve, Portugal*)
Lidia Puigvert-Mallart (*CREA-University of Barcelona, Spain*)
Daniel Schugurensky (*Arizona State University, USA*)
Joyce Stalker (*University of Waikato, Hamilton, New Zealand/Aotearoa*)
Juha Suoranta (*University of Tampere, Finland*)

VOLUME 25

The titles published in this series are listed at *brill.com/adul*

Pedagogies for Building Cultures of Peace

Challenging Constructions of an Enemy

By

Catherine Baillie Abidi

BRILL
SENSE

LEIDEN | BOSTON

Cover illustration: Marlon Solis

All chapters in this book have undergone peer review.

Library of Congress Cataloging-in-Publication Data

Names: Baillie Abidi, Catherine, author.
Title: Pedagogies for building cultures of peace : challenging constructions of an enemy / by Catherine Baillie Abidi.
Description: Leiden ; Boston : Brill Sense, [2018] | Series: International issues in adult education, ISSN 2352-2372 ; volume 25 | Includes bibliographical references and index. | Description based on print version record and CIP data provided by publisher; resource not viewed.
Identifiers: LCCN 2018025718 (print) | LCCN 2018032941 (ebook) | ISBN 9789004375239 (E-book) | ISBN 9789004375222 (hardback : alk. paper) | ISBN 9789004375215 (pbk. : alk. paper)
Subjects: LCSH: Peace--Study and teaching. | Peace-building--Study and teaching. | Other (Philosophy) | Hostility (Psychology) | Violence--Social aspects. | Young adults--Education--Social aspects.
Classification: LCC JZ5534 (ebook) | LCC JZ5534 .A28 2018 (print) | DDC 303.6/6--dc23
LC record available at https://lccn.loc.gov/2018025718

Typeface for the Latin, Greek, and Cyrillic scripts: "Brill". See and download: brill.com/brill-typeface.

ISSN 2352-2372
ISBN 978-90-04-37521-5 (paperback)
ISBN 978-90-04-37522-2 (hardback)
ISBN 978-90-04-37523-9 (e-book)

Copyright 2018 by Koninklijke Brill NV, Leiden, The Netherlands.
Koninklijke Brill NV incorporates the imprints Brill, Brill Hes & De Graaf, Brill Nijhoff, Brill Rodopi, Brill Sense and Hotei Publishing.
All rights reserved. No part of this publication may be reproduced, translated, stored in a retrieval system, or transmitted in any form or by any means, electronic, mechanical, photocopying, recording or otherwise, without prior written permission from the publisher.
Authorization to photocopy items for internal or personal use is granted by Koninklijke Brill NV provided that the appropriate fees are paid directly to The Copyright Clearance Center, 222 Rosewood Drive, Suite 910, Danvers, MA 01923, USA. Fees are subject to change.

This book is printed on acid-free paper and produced in a sustainable manner.

Contents

Acknowledgements IX
Introduction & Positionality X

1 Peacebuilding – Challenges & Opportunities 1

2 Understanding Violence 4
   1 Defining Violence 5
   2 Violence & Peace 7
   3 Constructions of an Enemy 8

3 The Interconnections of Violence, Peace & Power 11
   1 Understanding Power 12
   2 Power Frameworks 15

4 Educational Frameworks for Building Cultures of Peace 18
   1 Education for Peace – Foundational Perspectives 20
   2 Critical Adult Education & Education for Peace 20
   3 Contributions from Peacebuilding 23
   4 Contributions from International Humanitarian Law 24
   5 Intersections and Possibilities: Peace Work in Adult Education 25

5 Youth as Peacebuilders 28
   1 Young Adult Participants: Demographics & Relationships 32

6 Participatory, Critical and Collaborative Research *with* Youth 35
   1 Participatory and Collaborative Research – Inspirations from PAR 36
   2 Participatory and Collaborative Methodologies *with* Youth 36
   3 Methods: Pedagogical Processes 38
   4 Community Standards and Participation Processes 41
   5 PAR-Inspired Data Analysis 41
   6 Methodological Insights 42

7 Constructions of Enmity: Perspectives from Youth 44
   1 Constructions of Enmity 44
   2 Looking back, Learning together, Moving ahead: Key Insights from Professional Informants 56

3   Exploring Enmity Together – Collaborative Learning   60
 4   Conclusions and Discussions   63

8 Exploring Power Assumptions *with* Youth   65
 1   Power and Agency   65
 2   Power and Relations   66
 3   Power and Social Structure   68
 4   *Explicitly* Exploring Assumptions of Power Is Key for Collaborative Social Action   68
 5   Frameworks for Analyzing Power   69
 6   'The Onion' Analysis   70
 7   Expressions and Forms of Power   74

9 Strategies for Building Cultures of Peace *with* Youth   76
 1   The Goal: Building Cultures of Peace   77
 2   What is Needed for Cultures of Peace?   78
 3   Measuring Progress towards Cultures of Peace   79
 4   Respectful and Equitable Relations Are Building Blocks for Cultures of Peace   79
 5   Strategies for Cultures of Peace   80
 6   Empowered Individuals – Engaged Citizens   82
 7   Peaceful Relations   84
 8   Experiential Learning   84
 9   Discussion & Conclusions: Where Do We Go from Here?   86

10 Violence Transformation & Building Cultures of Peace   87
 1   Relational Approaches to Violence Transformation & Peacebuilding   88
 2   Relational, Peacebuilding Pedagogies   89
 3   Critical, Constructive and Relational Pedagogies for Peace   106
 4   Experiential Learning   112
 5   Sites for Peace Work within Adult Education   113
 6   Critical Adult Education and Violence Transformation: Concluding Thoughts   113

11 Peace, Pedagogy and Possibilities   115
 1   Research Significance   116
 2   Opportunities and Recommendations: Future Research and Practice   118
 3   Conclusion   120

Appendix 1: Guidelines for Photography 123
Appendix 2: Guidelines for Informal Conversations & Interviews with Young Adults 125
Appendix 3: Community Standards 126
Glossary 127
References 128
Index 141

Acknowledgements

For nearly twenty years I have had the opportunity to learn with youth, teachers, NGO colleagues, adult educators and humanitarian actors about peacebuilding possibilities in our globalized world. I am so grateful for these experiences and for the people who continue to open my eyes to new ways of living peacefully, together. I would especially like to thank the participants in this study and the Even Wars Have Limits volunteers for your passion to create a better, more peaceful world. It has been a privilege learning and creating with you.

Thank you to my family (especially Suz) for encouraging and supporting me and for your help at home. Thank you to my partner, Sohael, for your patience and for the late night tea deliveries as I worked. Thank you to my brother-in-law Sandy Matharu for bringing the youth's photographs to life in your drawings. And a special thank you to my children, Gian and Adli, for your understanding, your hugs, and for inspiring my peacebuilding research.

I would also like to thank Dr. John Gaventa, Dr. Susan Brigham and Dr. Mary Jane Harkins for your support, your thoughtful critiques, and your kindness. Finally, I would like to thank Dr. Elizabeth Lange. Your mentorship, encouragement, and critiques always came wrapped with humility and grace. Your practice speaks to your integrity as a person, a scholar and a teacher. I am so thankful to have been your student.

Introduction & Positionality

I have spent the past twenty years teaching and learning about the devastating consequences of war. I have learned about peace, conflict, and violence in post-conflict regions and in mine-affected communities. I have learned with regional and international humanitarian professionals, with teachers, with young Canadians, and with adult educators. I have also worked with, learned from, and provided support to people who have lived through horrendous journeys, including the loss of community, the loss of loved ones, and the loss of hope, all losses resulting from violence. My experience working within the Red Cross/Red Crescent Movement has exposed me to the diverse and devastating impacts of violence, but has also exposed me to a global humanity and collaborative resiliency. After years of working in the humanitarian field, I continue to question how we come to see someone as an enemy, as the *dehumanized other*, and this struggle deepens my commitment to creating and enacting peacebuilding strategies.

In addition to my humanitarian background, my research and practice are shaped by my identities as a white woman, an Anglophone, and a mother who comes from a middle-class family in a rural Maritime, Canadian community. My family is diverse with inter-generational, multi-ethnic, multi-lingual, multi-faith, and multi-citizenship statuses underpinning each other's lives. My personal values and limitations are both conscious and unconscious, and it is from this position that I pursue questions with Canadian young adults about enmity constructions, conflict transformations, and peacebuilding.

CHAPTER 1

Peacebuilding – Challenges & Opportunities

>What images come to mind when you hear the word violence?
>What images come to mind when you hear the word enemy?
>How do you learn to see someone as an enemy?

∴

Violence has been a constant reality throughout history and continues to be normalized as an innate part of the human experience. Enacted in multiple forms ranging from assault, to exploitation, to international armed conflict, violence penetrates our lives in many ways and in many spaces, both consciously and unconsciously. As violence pervades globally, accelerated by surging globalization[1] (Walby, 2009), competition for power and resources increases, national and corporate interests become increasingly privileged, fear is propagated, and securitization becomes the mechanism to confront adversity or conflict. Rooted firmly in securitized responses is the notion of the *dangerous other*, which is evident in exclusionary migration reforms (i.e. Trump's travel ban), in evolving militarized police tactics (i.e. Standing Rock), as well as in legislation to criminalize youth violence[2] such as bullying.

In the current Canadian climate of heightened attention on issues of violence, such as the highly publicized experiences of Amanda Todd[3] and Rehtaeh Parsons,[4] as well as the "Class of DDS 2015 Gentlemen" at the Dalhousie University Dentistry School,[5] it would appear that violence, particularly among youth, garners significant public attention. Yet, youth are rarely engaged in spaces or opportunities to shape social policy and practice, or recognized as having a significant role in conflict transformation (UNFPA, 2011; Podd, 2011; Toh, 2002). Additionally, the focus on reducing violence among youth largely fails to consider the wider social context in which youth live and interact, including the diverse power influences involved in maintaining normalizations of violence. Understanding how violence and dehumanization processes are constructed can contribute to the creation of peaceful practices. Collaborative research with youth,[6] exploring violence prevention, conflict transformation, and peace-centered processes are vital to building peaceful communities to ensure sustainable solutions for peace are possible.

While the impacts and increasing complexities of violence are widely documented (see WHO, 2014, 2016), spaces for critical dialogue about violence, opportunities for developing peaceful responses to the multiple forms and impacts of violence, and the implementation of violence prevention strategies are insufficient (WHO, 2014). Thus, the purpose of this book is to generate critical dialogue about violence as a means towards transforming normalizations of violence and building more peaceful communities. After all, "violence is preventable" (WHO, 2014).

Preventing violence requires substantial and sustained efforts in a multitude of areas, including health and education (WHO, 2014). Adult education offers an educational framework to shift how we currently understand and approach violence. In fact, Canadian adult education has always been connected to peace work and violence transformation, where aspirations for cooperative and equitable living were, and in many cases remain, centered. Organizations, such as the Canadian Voices of Women for Peace are an example of *negative peace* work (non-proliferation) within adult education whereby a rejection of violence, in all forms, is encouraged. Additionally, the work of the Canadian Council for International Cooperation and their member organizations, highlight the diversity of peace related programming and the far reach of community-based peace work in Canada. However, despite the historical context of peace education in Canada, peace work remains under-theorized within adult education. Additionally, shrinking public spaces for peace work as a result of reduced federal funding for civil society organizations, combined with increased neoliberal emphasis on economic growth at the expense of social and educational programming, heighten the need to maintain a focus on peace work within adult education. Furthermore, the influence of popular culture depicting unquestioned violations of human rights and normalizations of violence, intensifies the need for adult educators to enhance, reclaim and/or create learning spaces and practices for peace. Given the complexity of contemporary violence and the current deficit in peace-centered approaches to conflict, there is an eminent need for adult educators to engage more deeply in peace work, and to learn collaboratively with communities how peace processes and conflict transformation can be nurtured. Adult educators have a significant role to play towards building peaceful communities where equity is centered, where diverse voices are valued, including the voices of youth, and where conflict is embraced as an opportunity.

In this research study, using a critical and collaborative methodology, Canadian young adults reflect on and analyze how they construct the notion of an enemy (the *dehumanized other*), how power influences these constructions, and how pedagogies can be created toward building cultures of peace. Together, we incorporate their insights as well as insights shared by six experienced Canadian peace educators into the learning, dialogue and analysis processes examining normalizations of violence. While research has been conducted examining constructions of violence, few have done so collaboratively with youth, and even fewer have explored these issues collaboratively with youth who themselves were already engaged as peace educators among their peers. The findings from this study raise important questions about the normalization of violence, the role of power in teaching and learning about the relation between peace and violence, and the opportunities for young adult educators as agents for social change.

Notes

1 Globalization is defined diversely; however, Merriam (2010) suggests globalization can "be conceptualized as the movement of goods, services, and information across national boundaries" (p. 402). Globalization influences inequalities within the global economy and has a significant impact on the overall well-being of people, particularly people in the Global South (Walby, 2009; Weil, 2013).
2 Youth violence is defined by the WHO (2014) as "violence involving people between the ages of 10–29 years" (p. 84).
3 Amanda Todd committed suicide in 2012 as a result of sexualized violence and cyber bullying (Government of Canada, 2014). In 2017, a Dutch citizen was sentenced to 11 years for online fraud and blackmail. The same man will be extradited to Canada in 2018 to face charges of possession of child pornography, extortion, internet luring, criminal harassment, and distribution of child pornography in relation to Ms. Todd (CBC, 2017).
4 Rehtaeh Parsons committed suicide in 2013 as a result of sexualized violence and cyber bullying (CBC, 2014b). In 2015, two young men were charged in relation to Ms. Parsons: one for distributing child pornography; the other with the production of child pornography (CBC, 2015a).
5 In December 2014, Dalhousie University announced several female dentistry students had made a complaint under the university Sexual Harassment Policy in relation to on-line comments posted to a private Facebook group used by some of their male dentistry classmates (Dalhousie University, 2015). In January 2015, thirteen male dentistry students were suspended as a result of the on-going investigation of sex and gender based violence (Dalhousie University, 2015). A restorative justice process was utilized by Dalhousie University in response.
6 Due to the diverse interpretations of the transition period from childhood to adulthood and the overlap in age between UN definitions of youth and young adults, I used both terms throughout the book.

CHAPTER 2

Understanding Violence

> Unless treated, violence will be repeated.
> GALTUNG, *Peace by Peaceful Means: Peace and Conflict,*
> *Development and Civilization* (1996, p. 26)

∴

Globally, over 1.3 million people die annually as a result of violence and millions more suffer non-fatal consequences including social, emotional, physical, and economic consequences (WHO, 2014). Non-fatal consequences of violence can result in health problems, constraints on criminal justice systems, the erosion of community economies, and shattered interpersonal relations (WHO, 2014, 2016). The non-fatal consequences cause extraordinary social burden and are the most challenging to document (WHO, 2014). In this context, gender and sex based violence is widespread, considered to be at epidemic levels in Canada and internationally (Breire & Jordon, 2004; Price, 2005). Yet, it is significantly under reported. This may be due to a number of social and cultural barriers to reporting and inappropriate responses across a wide range of institutions – the undeniable impacts of sexism and patriarchy as a pervasive form of structural violence (WHO, 2014, 2016). Additionally, the depth of the impact of cyber related violence, such as cyberbullying, has only recently become validated as pervasive, particularly among youth. One in three Canadian youth report being cyber bullied, 25% report engaging in cyberbullying behavior, and 65% of those targeted have shared that their victimization has endured for over a year (Prevnet, 2015). The social and emotional impact of this emerging form of violence is immeasurable. Within the broad sphere of violence, the WHO (2014) argues young people "bear the burden" (p. 9).

Violence is a complex concept shaped by societies and the relations of power embedded within them. Violence is socially constructed and permeates interpersonal to international spaces (Walby, 2009). According to Walby (2009), "too often violence has been individualized as if it were the product of personal psychology and isolated failures of socialization; but it is not reducible to these" (p. 193). In fact, violence is inextricably linked with inequity (Bickmore, 2004; Pearce, 2009; Walby, 2009), and "strongly associated with social determinants such as weak governance; poor rule of law; cultural, social and gender norms; unemployment; income and gender inequality; rapid social change; and limited educational opportunities" (WHO, 2014, p. 33). Violence is also inextricably linked with conflict; however, it is important to distinguish these concepts as violence involves an intention to harm (Boulding, 1996). Distinguishing violence and conflict is an important foundation from which to begin exploring normalizations of violence.

In support of the notion that violence is a social construction, scientists from many regions of the world came together in 1986 to write the *Seville Statement on Violence* (UNESCO, 1986). Within this statement, these scientists argued five propositions to challenge the idea that humans have an inherent propensity for violence (UNESCO, 1986). The arguments highlighted how common justifications for violence, such as instinct and privileging aggressive behaviour are not scientifically validated. As stated by these scientists, "how we act is shaped by how we have been conditioned and socialized. There is nothing in our neurophysiology that compels us to react violently" (UNESCO, 1986, p. 2). Thus, unlike conflict, which is a natural part of human existence due to individual differences and limited resources (Boulding, 1996), interpersonal violence is preventable (WHO, 2014).

1   Defining Violence

Defining violence is a challenging endeavour considering the diversity of understandings that currently exist (Galtung, 1996; Pearce, 2007; WHO, 2002). Ongoing debates about what constitutes violence include perspectives from those who see violence as causing physical harm, to broader understandings, which include focusing on the conditions that allow suffering to occur (Galtung, 1996; Pearce, 2007; WHO, 2002). The WHO (2002) defines violence as

> the intentional use of physical force or power, threatened or actual, against oneself, another person, or against a group or community, that either results in or has a high likelihood of resulting in injury, death, psychological harm, maldevelopment, or deprivation. (p. 5)

Further to this definition, the WHO (2002) describes a typology of violence as occurring in three categories: self-directed, interpersonal, and collective (see Table 2.1).

The self-directed and interpersonal categories are typically portrayed as examples of violence. The collective violence category, however, is conceptually more challenging and is broken down into social, political, and economic

TABLE 2.1 World Health Organization – A typology of violence

	Self-directed		Interpersonal					Collective		
			Family/Partner			Community				
	Suicidal	Self-abuse	Child	Partner	Elder	Acquaintance	Stranger	Social	Political	Economic
Physical	x	x	x	x	x	x	x	x	x	x
Sexual			x	x	x	x	x	x	x	x
Psychological	x	x	x	x	x	x	x	x	x	x
Deprivation or neglect	x	x	x	x	x	x	x	x	x	x

(REPRINTED WITH PERMISSION FROM *WORLD REPORT ON VIOLENCE AND HEALTH*, WORLD HEALTH ORGANIZATION, 2002)

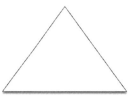

FIGURE 2.1 Violence triangle (Galtung, 1969)

entities. These sub-categories infer possible motive(s) for violence (WHO, 2002). For instance, social collective violence can include hate crimes; political collective violence can include state violence; and economic collective violence can include "attacks carried out with the purpose of disrupting economic activity, denying access to essential services, or creating economic division and fragmentation" (WHO, 2002, p. 6). The typology presented by the WHO (2002) demonstrates the pervasiveness of violence in society and the interconnections of "individual, relationship, social, cultural and environmental factors" (p. 12).

As opposed to the micro-macro typology of violence proposed by the WHO, Galtung (1996) suggested violence is better understood as *direct, structural,* and *cultural violence* also referred to as the *violence triangle* (see Figure 2.1) (Galtung, 1969, 1990, 1996). Within this model, *direct violence* includes behavioural acts of violence (physical or verbal, such as hitting or threatening); *structural violence* involves patterns of inequity (for example racism and sexism); and *cultural violence* is the attitudinal and belief processes that encourage direct and structural violence to manifest without question (religion or language for example). Galtung (1990) argued that *direct* and *structural violence* are often legitimized by *cultural violence,* which can be used to justify and make violence acceptable. This research study explicitly explores structural and cultural violence by analyzing normalizations of violence from the perspective of Canadian youth.

2 Violence & Peace

Violence and peace are woven together in a global public narrative that attempts to dictate the types of violence that are considered just or unjust depending on the actors creating the story (Butler, 2010; McLaren, 2005). Within this narrative, violence, including war, is often rationalized as necessary in the pursuit of peace (Butler, 2010; McLaren, 2005), which lies in direct contradiction to the United Nations (UN) approach to building a *culture of peace* (UN, 1998). In this regard, prominent peace educator Betty Reardon (1993) argued: "The central problem of peace is violence, in all its forms, at all levels of society" (p. 2).

The UN was created to prevent future wars and framed the concept of a *culture of peace* around the principles of the Charter of the UN (UN, 1998). Koichiro Matsuura, former director general of UNESCO, defined a *culture of peace* as "more than an absence of war ... it means justice and equity for all as the basis for living together in harmony and free from violence" (UNESCO, 2002, p. 1). In recognition of these indicators such as justice and equity, and in recognition of the many global instruments designed to promote peace and eliminate or reduce war as a particular manifestation of violence, it is imperative that we begin to critique violence, including state-led violence pitched in the name of peace (Butler, 2010). If patterns of violence are to be disrupted and transformed we need to better understand "how it has become so embedded" and normalized (Pearce, 2007, p. 9). We need to explore the normalizations of violence and not just the impacts (Zizek, 2008). It is in this regard that the youth involved in this research and I endeavored to deconstruct how we come to see another as less than human; how we construct the *dehumanized other*, the enemy.

3 Constructions of an Enemy

Constructions of *other*, particularly the *dehumanized* or *dangerous other*, are informed and shaped by complex social relations and are diversely understood. Popular culture, family and friends, cultural contexts, and formal schooling all contribute to how we come to understand violence and how we dehumanize *others* (Hakvoort & Oppenheimer, 1999; Shultz, 2012). Kaufman and Williams (2010) claim: "one of the basic tenants of conflict and the attendant violence directed at civilians that goes with it is the need to identify and isolate the 'other', specifically the group that becomes the enemy" (p. 37). These identity formations of self and other (I/You) evolve from and inside ideological frameworks, embodying past experiences with current contexts (Stamton & Swift, 1996, as cited in Mullaly, 2010; Tcherepashenets, 2011).

According to Galtung (1990), Gandhi challenged I/You constructions due to his belief that "any Self-Other gradient can be used to justify violence against those lower down on the scale of worthiness" (p. 302). Contemporary migration discourse from the Trump administration, serves as an example of how I/You identities, infused with securitization and radicalization, can reinforce the notion of the *dangerous other*. Othering linked with fear exists along a continuum of superiority and inferiority, and according to Shultz (2012), understanding *other* as inferior as opposed to *other* as different is a learned process of dehumanization. Spivak (1990) refers to this process of representation as the *epistemic violence* of *othering*, and exposes the politics embedded in representations of *other*.

The Latin origins of the term enemy, which infers 'not friend', is defined by hostility, harm or injury toward another (Enemy, 1995). The interconnections between othering and enmity are described by Galtung (1996) who argues "when Other is not only dehumanized but has been successfully converted into an 'it', deprived of humanhood, the stage is set for any type of direct violence, which is then blamed on the victim" (p. 203). Zizek (2008) similarly observes that the contemporary "tolerance towards others" is "counterpointed by an obsessive fear of harassment. In short, the Other is just fine, but only insofar as his (sic) presence is not intrusive, insofar as this Other is not really other" (p. 41).

Of equal importance in the process of reflecting on, critiquing and transforming constructions of identities and representations of *other*, are conversations about what in fact constitutes identity. Understanding the relationship between subjectivities[1] and the value of life or respect for human dignity are essential considerations for transforming violence. Butler (2010) proposes

> when the frames of war break up or break open, when the trace of lives is apprehended at the margin of what appears or as riddling its surface, then frames unwittingly establish a grievable population despite a prevalent interdiction, and there emerges the possibility of a critical outrage, war stands the chance of missing its mark. (p. xxx)

Seeing the identities of the *dehumanized other* from a humanitarian lens, while at the same time breaking the *frames* of violence that shape enmity constructions, are essential to understanding how value for life is designated. In this regard, Bhabha (1990) argues, "the 'other' is never outside or beyond us; it emerges forcefully, within cultural discourse" (p. 4). Said's (1978) *Orientalism* highlights this theoretical perspective of identity construction, or the construction of the *dangerous* or *dehumanized* other, which is produced through fabrication and representations developed within hegemonic discourses.

Giroux (1996) provides examples of this kind of hegemonically rooted identity construction, stating: "national identity, like nationalism itself, is a social construction that is built upon a series of inclusions and exclusions regarding history, citizenship, and national belonging" (p. 190). In this sense, identity constructions are influenced by historical and contextual factors, manifested by a discourse that continuously confuses descriptive and normative language; thus, further enabling ideological underpinnings to form our social constructions (Barker, 2008; Butler, 2010). In relation to the influences of past experiences and narratives, it is important to recognize the lack of neutrality in historical representations of *other* as well as the role of power and authority in the writing, teaching and learning of history (Hayward, 2013; Said, 2000). It is also important to acknowledge learning as a form of socialization that is rooted in hegemonic ways of knowing (Sawchuck, 2010).

Constructions of identity, particularly of enmity, are further complicated with diverse and contradictory ontologies.[2] "One of the ironies that comes to light is that groups of people can be the bitterest enemies in real life, yet ontologically they are on the same side; and a real-life ally can turn out to be one's ontological nemesis" (Lear, 2006, p. 50). For example, communities that share the same belief system, the same *truths* (for example, faith), may be engaged in violence. At the same time an ally to one of the parties of the conflict, who holds a contradictory ontology, may cause more harm in the long run. Western political and military actions in places such as Syria, Afghanistan, and Iraq serve as a prime example of this irony. Given this multiplicity of identities, people must come to value difference, embrace diverse identities, and practice non-violent approaches to conflict based on lived realities, to support the promotion of peace (Bickmore, 2006; Carr & Thesee, 2012).

The phenomenon of globalization significantly influences identity constructions and creates a continuous need for renewed identities (Tcherepashenets, 2011). Tcherepashenets (2011) argues the focus on renewal is "largely shaped by both the apparent geographic, cultural, and economic flexibility, which globalisation brings, and the reaction to it: the growing sense and even fear of insecurity" (Tcherepashenets, 2011, p. 192). Understanding how we learn to create a sense of otherness, which is often fused with representations of fear, is complicated by a lack of research that explores learning and identity constructions outside of formal schooling (Aberton, 2011). To address this gap, I examined processes leading toward dehumanization and enmity constructions with young adults engaged in peace education work within and beyond formal schooling, for the purpose of violence transformation and peacebuilding.

Notes

1 Subjectivity is defined by Barker (2008) as "the condition of being a person and the processes by which we become a person; that is, how we are constituted as subjects (biologically and culturally) and how we experience ourselves (including that which is indescribable)" (p. 215).
2 Study of being or becoming.

CHAPTER 3

The Interconnections of Violence, Peace & Power

> We need a concept broader than violence, and also broader than peace. Power is that concept.
> GALTUNG, *Peace by Peaceful Means: Peace and Conflict, Development and Civilization* (1996, p. 2)

∴

Understanding how power operates is integral to understanding how violence becomes normalized in society. According to Walby (2009), "violence is not merely an instrument or tool of already constituted power, it is itself constitutive of power ... violence is a form of power that is used to dominate others, to create fear and to shape their course of conduct" (p. 193). Although interconnected, power and violence are distinct, as Pearce (2013) argues: "dominating power still accepts that the other is an interlocutor, whose rights to physical existence is not in question. Violence on the other hand, questions that very right" (p. 2). Analyzing the role of power within the construction of enmity (or construction of the *dangerous* and *dehumanized other*) exposes how violence is fostered, sustained, and normalized, and how alternatives to violence can be constructed.

Power plays an essential role in the constructions of enmity, yet in Canada there is limited literature exploring the interrelations between learning, violence, and power. In two different studies exploring how children learn about violence and conflict in Canadian schools, Bickmore (2006) and Parker (2012) reveal a lack of explicit pedagogical focus on power influences in the overall curriculum documents and classroom experiences. Bickmore (2006) refers to this as "harmony themes" or a reluctance to engage in teaching and learning about controversial issues. Parker (2012) argues that cultures of peace can be nurtured by engaging in dialogic pedagogies, which seek to expose hidden curriculum and raise critical consciousness about power and inequities. Both Bickmore and Parker call for more research to explore the interrelations of power and conflict in learning contexts. While these studies were conducted in classroom settings with younger children, there are similar lessons to be learned in the field of adult education, and gaps to be narrowed in the literature exploring the intersection of violence, power and learning.

1 Understanding Power

Power is a complex, contentious, and relational concept (Gaventa, 2006), which is analyzed differently depending on the theoretical framework utilized. Each theoretical and methodological framework conveys different conceptions of power, for example there are structural perspectives, agency-centered perspectives, and power as intertwined within relationships and social norms. In relation to critical theories, power analyses tend to focus on access, control and domination. Power analyses from a post-structural perspective on the other hand, probe the intersections of power, knowledge and the discourses embedded within everyday living.

1.1 *Power and Structures*

Power from a structural view is seen as the "property of social structures and institutions" (Ng, 1995, p. 132), with the main unit of analysis being domination, or *power over* (Agger, 1991). Structural theorists aim to "draw attention to the relations of power that shape social reality" (Morrow, 1994, p. 59). The analysis of power from this perspective stems from critical theories (Barker, 2004; Freire, 2003; Hayward & Lukes, 2008). "Who has power, how it's negotiated, [and] what structures in society reinforce the current distribution of power" are questions that lie at the core of a structural analysis (Merriam, 2009, p. 35). Frameworks that are rooted in structural analyses of power, aim to expose dominant ideology, power imbalances, and to foster empowerment for the oppressed (Brookfield, 2005; Creswell, 2007; Freire, 1985; Guba & Lincoln, 1994). In relation to normalizations of violence, a structural analysis explores processes of inclusion and exclusion, processes which facilitate abundance for some and deficit for others, and processes of manipulation that seek to make inequitable systems invisible, particularly to those most directly affected.

Hayward (2000) contends that power exists in the form of socialized norms; her argument stems from a structural analysis. "De-facing power" as she calls it, "is a matter of conceptualizing political mechanisms as boundaries ... that facilitate and limit action for all actors, in all social contexts" (Hayward, 2000, p. 8). Hayward (2000) suggests mechanisms of power include laws and norms, and while she acknowledges agency, she critiques agent-centered power analyses due to the constraints on some people to "have agency," the social origins of these constraints, and thus recognizing "that they are constrained in ways they need not be" (Hayward & Lukes, 2008, p. 15). Hayward (in Hayward & Lukes, 2008) claims that

> as agents act and interact within structural limits, they develop expectations about what it is that one does, and what it is that one ought to do, in particular contexts. They develop not just subjective, but also intersubjective, understandings of the meanings particular actions hold. These social expectations and social meanings always mediate between, on the one hand, structural constraints (such as laws, policies, rules, or norms), and on the other hand, the action and the inaction of human agents. Structure does not determine action. Instead, it *shapes* action, by rendering some forms, in some contexts, costly or otherwise difficult, while rewarding or otherwise encouraging others. Structure shapes social action *through* social meanings, which agents continually interpret and re-interpret. (p. 14)

In this sense, power is contained in societal boundaries and not necessarily within agents (Hayward, 2000). Power is therefore "tied to agency acting within and upon structures" (Hayward & Lukes, 2008, p. 14).

1.2 *Power and Agency*

Although some feminist methodologies focus on "structured power relations and interlocking systems of oppression based on gender, race, class, age, and so on," others add another layer of analysis by drawing attention to personal power and agency (Tisdell, 1993, p. 94). An agency analysis centers on the ability of the oppressed to overcome oppression and resist dominant thinking based on their experiences (Tisdell, 1993) in a self-productive manner (Gore, 1992).

Agency is connected to *power to* and *power with*, two concepts that focus on the capacity for resistance and collective action (Barker, 2004; Hayward, 2006; Veneklasen & Miller, 2002). Power as agency focuses on the capabilities for resistance and action in situations of social inequity (Gore, 1992). The main unit of analysis for power as agency is the subject.

Lukes' (1974, 2005) third face of power is an example of an agency-based power analysis focused on exposing internalized concessions to domination. Within this third face or dimension, the primary focus is on the agent(s), regardless of intention or action for the purpose of "blame or reward"

(Hayward & Lukes, 2008). Lukes (in Hayward & Lukes, 2008) focuses heavily on the need for accountability and for those in power to be responsible for their actions. Lukes (2008) further argues that "human agents, whether individuals or collectives, have power or are powerful within structural limits, which enable and constrain their power" (in Hayward & Lukes, p. 12). Gaventa (1980, 2006) builds on Lukes' work to consider the *internalization of powerlessness*, a look beyond the hidden forms of power to include a focus on learned helplessness. An agency-centered power analysis exploring enmity constructions focuses on the 'who' in terms of access, resources, and abilities/freedoms to act.

1.3 *Power and Socializations*

Countless frameworks and conceptions of power challenge both a structural and agential analysis. Foucault (1979), for instance, claimed that power is everywhere, manifested as complex sets of relationships, which are fluid, forever changing, and learned. "For Foucault, power is a relation not a possession or a capacity" (Orner, 1992, p. 77). Foucault (2000) critiqued structural perspectives of power, which privilege the role of the state, and instead argued:

> relations of power, and hence the analysis that must be made of them, necessarily extend beyond the limits of the state – in two senses. First of all, because the state for all the omnipotence of its apparatuses, is far from being able to occupy the whole field of actual power relations; and, further, because the state can only operate on the basis of the other, already-existing power relations. (p. 122)

Similarly, Francis (2010) suggested, "if power is the ability to create something, to make something happen or to influence or change something or someone, this may be achieved in many different ways and through many different kinds of relationships" (p. 114).

Foucault (1982) argued that power is productive and the focus of analyses should be on the resistance to power "to bring to light power relations, locate their positions, and find out their point of application and the methods used" (p. 780). Integral to Foucault's (1982) notion of power is the interconnection between power and knowledge. According to Foucault, "power relations do not simply distort knowledge ... rather knowledge itself is rooted in power relations" (cited in Morrow, 1994, p. 135); thus the "acquisitions" and "transmissions" of knowledge and power are inextricably linked (Foucault, 2000). From a Foucauldian perspective, action centers around challenging socialized norms. A discourse analysis is an example of resistance whereby text is explored to uncover who is speaking and which perspectives are being reproduced and normalized. Lear (2006) suggests in this capacity, "the issue that concerns us is not who has the power to tell the story – however important that might be; it is rather how power shapes what any true story could possibly be" (p. 31).

Hayward's (2013) power analysis examining socialized norms (interconnections between agency and structure) also shares fundamental synergies with Foucault's ideas around resistance. For instance, Hayward (2013) argues that the emphasis of our analysis should not be how "narratives were told and retold, but how they were institutionalized and how they were objectified in the physical spaces" (p. 45). Analyzing power from this perspective enables an exploration of how stories (of enmity in this case) have become rooted in our everyday lives.

Jackson (2011) argues power "exists within all (local and global) social structures and interactions, and people respond to it, exercise it or resist it according to social, cultural, political and educational contexts, and within constructs of difference" (p. 285). Similarly, Mayo (1999) suggests that power ought not to be considered as "things" but rather "complex sets of social relations" (p. 26). From this stance, power is not the property of individuals or structures but rather a complex relationship between the two (Conti & O'Neil, 2007).

2 Power Frameworks

Understandings and debates about power continue to evolve and change, thus the frameworks to analyze how power operates also evolve. Mohanty (2003) argues power cannot be considered in binaries, such as the powerful and the powerless, but rather that it can be regarded as fluid and simultaneously existing in different ways and at different spatial and temporal locations. In this regard, Hayward and Lukes (2008) discuss the risks involved in power analyses stemming from just one theoretical framework:

> If we think of power, as Lukes urges us, in strictly agent-centric terms, then we may overlook some subset of significant and remediable social constraints on human freedom. Nevertheless, if we think of power, as Hayward suggests, in structural terms, then we may lose sight of those particular agents who are responsible for the constraints we analyze and review. (p. 17)

Thus, if power is understood as being fluid and contextualized within time, space and relationships, then analyzing power requires a multifaceted framework.

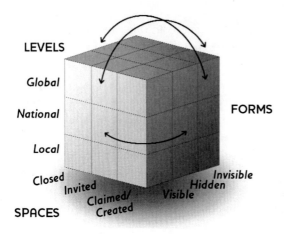

FIGURE 3.1   Gaventa's power cube (from Gaventa, 2007, reprinted here with permission)

Numerous frameworks exist to analyze power, each yielding a different lens for critique and exploration. For instance, Gaventa's (2007) *Power Cube* (see Figure 3.1) was designed as a community tool for analyzing the levels (regional, national, and international), forms (visible, hidden, and invisible) and spaces (closed, invited, and claimed/created) of power. The *Power Cube* is primarily an agent-centered tool of analysis, which links agency and structure while emphasizing the interrelations of power (Gaventa, 2007). Pantazidou (2012) described the *Power Cube* as a framework to explore "forms, spaces and levels of power that enable and constrain action; however it does not invite an explicit focus on actors and their relationships" (p. 9). Pantazidou (2012) thus argued the *Power Cube* could be used with an actor/network analysis to enhance the overall analysis.

Recognizing the complexity of power, emergent understandings, and the limits of the *Power Cube*, Gaventa (2006) welcomes additional perspectives and reconfigurations in his presentation of the *Power Cube*. Most reconfigurations maintain an agency lens, such as the *Expressions of Power*, which are described by Veneklasen and Miller (2000, p. 45) as *power over* (domination); *power to* (individual action); *power with* (collective action); and *power within* (self-worth). Additional lenses include a gendered perspective exploring power in public, private, and intimate spaces (Veneklasen & Miller, 2002). Other frameworks, such as Hayward's (2000) notion of 'de-facing power,' argue that key areas of a power analysis should be centered, such as the critical exploration into *invisible powers*. *Invisible powers*, according to Gaventa (1980), are the internalized understandings of the status quo, particularly internalized powerlessness, that overtime have become 'unseeable.' In this way, invisible powers are deeply embedded (unconscious) mechanisms for maintaining hegemony, which is the "process by which one group convinces another that being subordinate is a desirable state of affairs" (Brookfield, 2005, p. 98). In relation to 'unseeable power' and hegemony, Gaventa and Cornwall (2007) contend "if power is shaped by discourse, then questions of how discourses are formed, and how they shape the fields of action, become central for changing and affecting power relations" (p. 176). Thus, critical analyses on constructions of enmity and normalizations of violence need to move beyond merely the operation of hidden power, to an investigation of where and how invisible forms of hegemonic power operate and thrive.

CHAPTER 4

Educational Frameworks for Building Cultures of Peace

> Education is at the heart of any strategy for peace-building. It is through education that the broadest possible introduction can be provided to the values, skills and knowledge which form the basis of respect for human rights and democratic principles, the rejection of violence, and a spirit of tolerance, understanding and mutual appreciation among individuals, groups and nations.
> UNESCO, *Strategy on human rights 1996–2001*, 1995

∴

Numerous frameworks exist aiming to prevent or reduce violence, and develop peaceful processes. These frameworks approach peace and conflict from many angles, including from *negative* or *positive peace* frames. What constitutes peace, peaceful practices, and cultures of peace, will invariably depend on the storyteller and the context in which the story is being told, as peace is culturally, spatially, and temporally informed. Although a universal vision of a culture of peace is not plausible, there are common peace values and principles, such as respect for human dignity, which inform peace work. The challenge prevails in the practice of building cultures of peace when visions and implementation strategies are confounded in the complexity that is real life.

"Peace societies for much of the past century have depended on education to alert young and old, men and women, to the international structures and systematic inequalities that encourage militarism and discourage peaceful solutions" (Cook, 2008, p. 894). Educational frameworks for building cultures of peace have been shaped by the Frankfurt School scholars, peace educators such as Galtung and Reardon, and many others who have sought to better understand peace and to transform the proliferation war. Elements of this work are found in multi-cultural education, anti-racist education, and development education – to name a few. In fact, learning how to shift "cultural and social norms that support violence" is one of the seven violence prevention strategies[1] purported by the WHO (2014, p. viii).

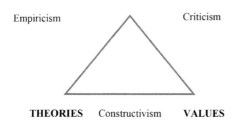

FIGURE 4.1   Galtung's peace epistemologies (from Galtung, 1996, reprinted with permission)

In an effort to develop a framework for teaching and learning peaceful processes, Galtung (1996) articulated three peace epistemologies[2]: empirical peace, critical peace, and constructive peace (see Figure 4.1). Galtung (1996) claimed *empirical peace* privileges data to "reveal patterns and conditions for peace" in order to improve theories for peace (Galtung, 1996, p. 9). *Critical peace* emphasizes the relationship between data and values, while exposing opportunities for change based on critiques of the systems and structures that maintain peacelessness (Galtung, 1996). Finally, *constructive peace* merges theories of change with peace values (Galtung, 1996). Galtung's (1996) peace epistemologies provide a framework to explore teaching and learning for peace and a foundation from which to understand peace processes. Understanding the epistemologies of peace is essential to building cultures of peace, as this enables a framework to consider how peace operates (or ought to operate) within society.

In addition to Galtung's (1996) peace epistemologies, Thayer-Bacon (2003) argues in favour of a relational epistemology where knowing develops within and among relations. Thayer-Bacon (2003) argues how we come to know, in this case peace or processes for building peace, must include an appreciation for diverse experiences and social contexts. According to Thayer-Bacon (2003),

> A relational (e)pistemology emphasizes the transactional nature of knowing in a variety of ways. Most important, it emphasizes the connections knowers have to the known and helps us understand that we are not spectators to reality reporting on "it"; we are of this work, this universe, affecting "it" as we experience "it". (p. 79)

Using relational epistemologies in combination with Galtung's (1996) *constructive peace* epistemology, as discussed above, provides a framework to contextualize peace within the everyday interactions of people. Privileging the interrelationships between theories of change, peace values, and relational epistemologies may enable future manifestations for peace.

1. Education for Peace – Foundational Perspectives

Education for peace and conflict transformation has a long history within Canadian public education, particularly after World War II. A review of Canadian curricular outcomes, especially at the lower elementary level, reveals the lasting impact of the post-World War II peace sentiment. Children in Canada are learning about healthy relationships, human rights, empathy, and some are practicing mindfulness within the classroom as a particular strategy toward inner peacefulness. External organizations are also providing support to teachers and schools in the area of peace education. For example, Peaceful Schools International, an organization focused on providing "children with the tools they need to live well with others," was created in Nova Scotia to support the creation of cultures of peace within schools (Peaceful Schools International, 2015). Peaceful Schools International works with over 350 member schools around the world utilizing a comprehensive peace education approach.

While much peace work has been done and continues to be done within Canadian schools, peace related education is rarely supported by a theoretical framework, or specifically aligned with peace epistemologies as argued by Galtung. Bickmore (2011) argues that peace education in Canadian schools is not comprehensive, many barriers exist within school systems preventing a comprehensive approach, and schools tend to spend more time and resources on surveillance activities as opposed to peacebuilding. Furthermore, the links between public school peace-related education and adult education oriented toward conflict transformation are largely unrecognized or supported.

2. Critical Adult Education & Education for Peace

Adult education is a vast field with diverse understandings and meanings, but its roots, at least in the Western context, are undeniably situated in a pursuit for social justice (English & Mayo, 2012; Jackson, 2011; Merriam, 2010; Nesbit, 2013). Stemming from critical social theory, critical adult education aims to expose and critique unjust and inequitable social structures and ideologies. In this sense, critical education enables the roots of violence to be examined by focusing on resistance and contradictions with the purpose being a deep analysis of social inequality, a process epistemologically linked to Galtung's critical peace. Furthermore, critical educational research "queries the context where learning takes place, including the larger systems of society, the culture and institutions that shape educational practice, and the structural and historical conditions framing practice" (Merriam, 2009, p. 35). Thus, the dual focus on process and content within critical adult education provides a useful frame for this study due to the focus on power and violence, and the participatory processes employed. Centering questions of power, voice and hegemony while engaging in participatory and community-based learning processes are important dimensions of peace work.

Freire (2003) argued critical education is a process of "learning to perceive social, political, and economic contradictions and to take action against the oppressive elements of reality" (p. 35). For Freire (1970), critical education is about hope, liberation, and social justice through a process of *critical consciousness,* particularly within marginalized communities. The exploration of how power influences the construction of enmity and how learning opportunities can be created to challenge these constructions within the critical paradigm, frames the focus on analyzing power and learning with oppressed and discriminated populations (Mertens, 2009), in this case, youth. While youth are a heterogeneous group, they are largely marginalized from spaces of policy development and implementation, and are rarely engaged in democratic governance structures in positions of real participation (Giroux, 1996; UNESCO, 2004; Warner, Langlois, & Dumand, 2010). Youth, as a general group, are organized as *other* in society (Orner, 1992). Therefore, learning with youth to challenge and transform enmity constructions fits well in a critical pedagogical process. After all, critical education, including critical pedagogy, is a form of social transformation through education (Wink, 2011).

Giroux's (1993) *Pedagogy of representation* offers a particular critical pedagogical approach to violence transformation. He suggests that the pedagogy of representation

> focuses on demystifying the act and process of representing by revealing how meanings are produced within relations of power that narrate identities through history, social forms, and modes of ethical address that appear objective, universal, valid, and consensual. (Giroux, 1993, p. 114)

Giroux argues that education in this area requires a review of history, educator resistance from engaging with oppressive representations, and an exploration of how power influences representations. Specifically, his pedagogy of representation calls for a *re-writing* process which embraces the following key questions: who is benefiting from "the representations in question; where can we situate such representations ethically and politically with respect to questions of social justice and human freedom; what moral, ethical and ideological principles structure our reactions to such representations" (Giroux, 1993, p. 118). Using Giroux's pedagogy of representation as a pedagogical process to explore constructions of enmity can provide opportunities to make invisible forms of power visible, and help to identify possibilities for peace work.

While critical education offers plausible pedagogies for peace work, there are important limitations and critiques to consider. Early critiques of critical pedagogy came from feminist scholars who highlighted a lack of gendered analysis (Ellsworth, 1992; Lewis, 1992; Luke & Gore, 1992; Tisdell, 1993), a lack of racial analysis (hooks, 2003; Tisdell, 1993), and a concern about the power assumed in the role of teacher (Ellsworth, 1992; Rezow-Rashi, 1995; Zingaro, 2009). Teachers may be unprepared for their role as critical pedagogues, and as a result, promote hegemonic narratives (or stories) (Bohan, Doppen, Feinberg, & O'Mahony, 2008). Ellsworth (1992) suggested, "critical pedagogues are always implicated in the very structures they are trying to change" (p. 107). Feminist scholars also challenge the possibility of emancipating others and question whose idea of social justice is being pursued and prescribed by critical pedagogy (Ellsworth, 1992; Lather, 1992; Lewis, 1992). These critiques offer valuable insights for reflection and reflexivity. In this study, reflexivity and the collaborative learning approach are important elements, designed to reduce the teacher-student duality and, instead, embrace a collaborative learning community where the learning context is acknowledged, critiqued, and explored.

Furthermore, research and practice in the area of peace and conflict transformation is unsystematic within adult education. Formal post-secondary programs focusing on peace and conflict exist within varying disciplines such as political science; however, rarely are these programs linked with faculties of education/adult education. Even though there are Canadian adult educators doing important and creative work in the areas of anti-racist, multicultural, and peace education (see Dei, Abdi, Toh, Brigham, for example), the field lacks a comprehensive, cohesive, and collaborative approach to peace work. Furthermore, despite a rich history of community-based peace work, for instance Voices of Women for Peace, the Pugwash Movement, and the Tatamagouche Centre, learning opportunities focused on peacebuilding are vanishing due to shifting policy priorities and decreased federal funding to community sectors and non-governmental organizations (NGOs). The reduction and centralization of NGO offices, such as centralization of Canadian University Services Overseas (CUSO), and the closure of the Pearson Center for peacekeeping in 2013, are examples of this reduced federal support for cooperative and peace work. Yet, despite the lack of peace work in adult education today, the diversity of spaces where adult education is occurring, the community-based processes which are supported, and the critical foundation of the field, creates enormous opportunity for engaging people and communities in building cultures of peace.

3 Contributions from Peacebuilding

The concept of peacebuilding has evolved from a focus on physical security and direct action in conflict-affected regions, to include comprehensive and coordinated strategies involving civil society, government, humanitarian actors, and many nontraditional sectors (Schirch, 2013). Bickmore (2004) contends that peacebuilding is the "redress of underlying inequities and social conflicts to restore healthy relationships and/or prevent future escalations of conflicts" (p. 77). In this regard, peacebuilding includes activities oriented toward structural and cultural peace (Galtung, 1996); processes that require a sustained commitment to reflection, flexibility, and community-centered engagement (Stephenson & Zanotti, 2012; Zelizer & Rubinstein, 2009); and an alignment of "our heads and our hearts" (Collin Marks & Marks, 2002, p. 19).

Peacebuilding education is an extension of peacebuilding into the realm of teaching and learning, embracing a focus on social justice and peaceful citizenship. According to Bush and Saltarelli (2000), peacebuilding education is a form of peace education, although with a deeper emphasis on challenging structural causes of violence. This claim speaks to Galtung's (1983) concern about the limitations of peace education:

> peace education has to be concerned not only with the projection of images of the horrors of war, the suffering and the costs (easily done), and images of the delights of peace, the enjoyment and the benefits (more difficult, as this is ordinary life, this thing referred to as 'peace', which means that real peace studies have to have a tinge of the utopian about them, to go further than non-war – that is, beyond data and into the realm of imagination). Peace education has also to be concerned with what to do about it, which means that there has to be not only a theory of how to avoid war and build peace, but a 'do-able' theory, linked to some kind of practice for those who study this field. (p. 283)

Peacebuilding education embraces conflict as a naturally occurring reality and extends beyond the emphasis on data assessment (epistemological peace), and embraces a relational epistemology, where the restoration of compromised relations is paramount. Peacebuilding education is an interdisciplinary approach focused on reducing inequities, whereby the voices of those directly affected by violence are central, strategies for change are generated within and by grassroots communities in the context of everyday experience, and the development of healthy relations is considered the ultimate goal (Bush & Saltarelli, 2000). Thus, peacebuilding education is focused on the opportunity within conflict for long-term social change (conflict transformation) as opposed to fixing the 'problem' of conflict (conflict resolution). According to Lederach (2006) this kind of social change or conflict transformation, is centered on relationships. He further argues,

> conflict transformation is to envision and respond to the ebb and flow of social conflict as life giving opportunities for creating constructive change processes that reduce violence, increase justice in direct interaction and social structures, and respond to real-life problems in human relationships. (p. 26)

As previously described, there are strengths within peacebuilding; however, there are challenges as well. For example, the tensions that exist between human security and national security impact how and when peacebuilding strategies are implemented. Similarly, peacebuilding as an approach to peace work is accepted differently, depending on the community context (Schirch, 2013). Finally, the interdisciplinarity of peacebuilding increases the complexity of the work. At the same time, the dual approach of peacebuilding education, embracing both positive and negative peace, offers a comprehensive strategy for mitigating the impact of violence while building cultures of peace.

4   Contributions from International Humanitarian Law

Laws prohibiting violence are common and they aim to reinforce acceptable behaviours and promote respect (WHO, 2014). Within public international law, international humanitarian law (IHL) is the minimum threshold of accepted violence within armed conflict. IHL fits within the grand narrative of peace and conflict and operates under the assumption that war and armed violence will remain a permanent reality. IHL is a harm reduction approach, which aims to limit behaviour during armed conflict but not prohibit violence all together. The levels and forms of violence authorized during armed conflict, often referred to as the means and methods, depend on issues of proportionality (collateral damage vs. military advantage) and distinction (combatant vs. non-combatant). Furthermore, IHL does not focus on why violence may occur; it merely provides guidelines indicating when and how violence can be enacted (Greenberg Research, 1999; Fresard, 2004).

IHL is embedded within a treaty system and the corresponding educational approaches have placed significant weight on the adherence to the universally ratified 1949 Geneva Conventions. Education on the rules of IHL have traditionally focused on dissemination, assuming increased awareness will result in adherence to the rule of law and reduced suffering during armed conflict. Contemporary IHL education has evolved to focus beyond awareness of the rules, to include emphasis on mitigating retribution and enhancing respect for others. In this regard, IHL education connects with Galtung's (1996) constructive peace, as the values of respect for human dignity are aspired within a legal framework dictating acceptable behavior in times of armed conflict.

The WHO (2014) argues "the enactment and enforcement of legislation on crime and violence are critical for establishing norms of acceptable and unacceptable behaviour, and creating safe and peaceful societies," and yet, the enforcement of these laws are lacking (p. 38). This critique is true of IHL as well. Enforcement for violations of IHL are the responsibility of the States who are party to the Geneva Conventions and efforts to hold those responsible for violations vary from country to country and from conflict to conflict. Additionally, IHL falls within a negative peace agenda and falls short in inspiring a culture of non-violence. Galtung (1969) argues the priority of a negative peace agenda involves the elimination of war-related means and methods, assuming that a focus on non-proliferation will result in a non-war culture. By focusing on maintaining "a bare minimum threshold of humanity," IHL does little to transform social normalizations of violence or to prevent a return to violence following war activity.

5 Intersections and Possibilities: Peace Work in Adult Education

> In a post-September 11 world marked by growing political and cultural conflict and Terror War, education must also address the problems of war and conflict and make human rights education, peace education and the solving of conflicts through mediation an important part of a democratic curriculum. Critical Pedagogy must engage the difficult issue of overcoming differences, understanding cultures very dissimilar from one's own, and developing a more inconclusive democracy that will incorporate marginalized groups and resolve conflicts between diverse groups and cultures. (Kellner, 2005, p. 66)

Globalization is changing social landscapes and as a result, Apple (2011) argues a different kind of education is required. Moving from transactional to transformational social engagement, from empowered individuals to empowered and inclusive communities, from communications to critical conversations, and from taking action to solidarity, all elements to building cultures of peace, requires complex theoretical approaches (MCIC, 2013).[3] Given this complexity, transdisciplinary and intersectional[4] approaches are necessary to transform violence (Walby, 2009). The interconnections between identity constructions, power influences, and violence is more comprehensively explored in a merging of critical and post-structural theoretical frames where critique, power, and voice are privileged within a plurality of truths. In this regard, Kincheloe (2009) argues that epistemologically, there has never been a universal cultural or historical understanding of knowledge and learning. Thus,

> knowing this, we can operate in a far more humble domain, become more insightful about the forces that shape our own and other people's constructions of reality, gain the ability to understand the dynamics that limit our understandings, appreciate the value of other people's and other culture's ways of seeing, and discern how to avoid the pitfalls of reductionism. (Kincheloe, 2009, p. 111)

By understanding how power influences constructions of enmity, further insight into how we can challenge these constructions and nurture peaceful processes can be discovered.

Critical adult education (including critical pedagogy), peacebuilding education, and international humanitarian law, offer important strategies toward building cultures of peace. Ontologically, they share common truths, namely the inevitability of conflict and goals to reduce the impact of violence. Epistemologically, they differ in how data, theory, values, and relations are privileged. At the same time, these epistemological differences highlight opportunities to reconsider how knowledge is constructed. By exploring the interconnections of critical adult education, humanitarian law, and peacebuilding education, the dualistic notions of individual and society, and agency and structure can be reimagined to consider a spectrum of relations in which conflict and/or violence occur. In this framework, all dimensions of conflict transformation, as described by Schirch (2013), are considered including: personal, relational, cultural, and structural levels, which are immersed within a power analysis.

A theoretical framework for building peace that embraces positive and negative peace processes, in combination with diverse epistemologies, challenges educators to deepen the theorization of their practice. Given the complexity of violence today and the increased Canadian prioritization on securitization versus peacebuilding, it is imperative that transdisciplinary and intersectional approaches to building peace are adopted (Walby, 2009). Infusing the treaty-based, harm reduction approach of humanitarian law (negative peace), with the relationship building and conflict transformation aims of peacebuilding (negative and positive peace), in combination with the participatory practice and ideology critiques of critical adult education can create a new framework for conceptualizing transformations for peace. In this regard, the implications for adult education are extensive. Adult educators have an essential role to play in building a culture of peace.

Notes

1 The seven strategies for violence prevention/reduction as identified by the WHO (2014) include: (1) a focus on healthy parent-child relations; (2) "developing life skills in children and adolescents"; (3) limiting alcohol (availability and "harmful use"); (4) "reducing access to guns and knives"; (5) the promotion of gender equality; (6) challenging normalizations of violence; and, (7) support for victims of violence (p. viii).
2 Epistemology is the study of knowledge.
3 The transitions discussed were created by a national working group contributing to the development of a toolkit on public engagement on international development issues. The toolkit was developed for the Canadian Council for International Cooperation and provincial Councils.
4 Intersectionality "is a term to describe the relationship between multiple forms of social inequality" (Walby, 2009, p. 60).

CHAPTER 5

Youth as Peacebuilders

> All over the world, youth are driving social change and innovation, claiming respect for their fundamental human rights and freedoms, and seeking new opportunities to learn and work together for a better future.
>
> UNESCO, *Empowering youth through national policies*, 2004

∴

Defining what constitutes childhood and/or adulthood is influenced by cultural, temporal, and spatial considerations (Barker, 2008; UNESCO, 2004; Wlodkowski, 2008). UNESCO (2004) describes *youth* as a multifaceted

> stage between childhood and adulthood, when people have to negotiate a complex interplay of both personal and socio-economic changes in order to maneuver the 'transition' from dependence to independence, take effective control of their own lives and assume social commitments. (p. 5)

According to UNESCO (2004), youth are persons between the ages of 15–24 and there are one billion youth in the world, accounting for 18 percent of the global population (UNESCO, 2004). While youth are often defined by their age (or stage), they are a heterogeneous group of people with diverse identities, experiences, and lived realities. Davies (2010) argues the diversity of youth include "differences in the material conditions of their lives; in how they see and define themselves; in how they are seen by others (including other young people); in how they are treated by others, both in their personal contacts and by organizations and institutions" (p. 4). Educational frameworks that respond to this complexity provide a stronger foundation from which to explore social learning processes related to conflict transformation. Yet, youth are largely missing within adult education research and practice. The lack of perspectives from youth highlights a failure within adult education to value learning across the lifespan and to acknowledge and support transitions occurring from childhood to adulthood.

While youth are a heterogeneous group of people, diverse in experience and perspective, the everyday lives of youth include unique influences and power relations that are in many ways, different than their older adult counterparts. The complexities of violence, as experienced by youth, are complicated by biological and sociocultural factors, including popular cultural influences. Youth today are learning in uncertain times, where decreased family engagement (Barker, 2008), decreased employment, increasing economic disparity (UNESCO, 2004) and broken public schooling are shaping their lived reality (Giroux, 2011). Social media and rapidly advancing technologies are also informing and influencing the lives of youth. Furthermore, youth are regularly organized as *other* in academic literature and mainstream discourse (Giroux, 1996; Orner, 1992) and are highly associated with risky behaviour, criminality, and violence (Giroux, 1996; Ramberg, 2003). A search of federal documents on the topic of Canadian youth results in two key discourses: health and criminality (Statistics Canada, 2013b). In a Canadian context, the evidence does not support an increase in youth crime yet the narrative of youth and criminality is well established (Bickmore, 2011). Understanding the cultural context, in which youth are learning and teaching about violence and enmity, is an essential piece of the picture when exploring transformations in enmity constructions and the normalization of violence.

Despite increasing narratives about deviant youth, regionally and globally, youth are described as having a vital role in bringing societal change (ICRC, 2011; UNESCO, 2004, 2011). According to UNESCO (2004),

> Between 1989 and 2000, 111 armed conflicts were reported in the world involving 300,000 child and youth soldiers[1] fighting in 49 countries. There is no conflict without youth participation; indeed, young men constitute the majority of armed forces in most countries. There is a pressing need to strengthen efforts by young people to build peace and promote a general culture of peace. (p. 19)

Youth are connected to violence and peace, directly and indirectly, and these experiences are essential to understanding violence and peace from regional to global contexts.

Nabavi and Lund (2010) argue youth often have a greater consciousness of global issues than adults and they are "better able to mobilize peers, communicate effectively using innovative technological tools, and locate and evaluate information on issues more quickly from a wide variety of sources" (p. 7). For instance, Giroux (2011) argues that many European youth are challenging political leadership to ensure participation in the democratic process. Giroux (2011) further contends that today's youth are "fighting back and, in doing so, inventing new pedagogical tools to expose the official scripts of power while at the same time constructing new modes of association and struggle based on democratic ideals and values" (p. 331). The youth engaged in the Occupy, Maple Spring, and Idle No More movements are strong Canadian examples of the ability of youth to engage in peace work and to create social change. At the same time, Giroux (2011) questions why youth in America are not participating and resisting similar oppressions; particularly considering that youth participation is not holistically practiced in governance, social structures, or community development (Giroux, 1996; UNESCO, 2004; Warner, Langlois, & Dumand, 2010).

UNESCO's (2004) youth policy argues for the "comprehensive involvement and appropriate decision-taking of youth at all levels, including communities, schools and universities at the provincial and national level" (p. 14). Apple (2005) similarly encourages communities to make visible models for youth engagement that value the capacity of youth to lead change and contribute to new ways of knowing and doing. He argues for the creation of "alliances that begin to cut across race, class, and age," include the "real participation" of youth, and focus on learning and challenging neoliberal notions of democracy to instead create alternative models for "living our freedoms" (Apple, 2005, p. 105). Encouraging youth voice as the quintessential focus in youth engagement, where concerns of youth are respected, and where adults serve in a support and mentorship role, is essential for imagining alternative ways toward a peaceful future (Children and Youth in Challenging Contexts Network, 2014a; DeKraai, Bulling, McLean, & Fletcher, 2010; Jones & Yonezawa, 2010). "Our communities will only reach their potential as vibrant and healthy places when youth are welcomed as full participating members" (Warner, Langlois, & Dumond, 2010, p. 95).

Lindeman (1937, as cited in Briton, 1996) maintained that "social justice cannot be achieved through the learning of children and youth ... the young make their adaptations to an adult-controlled world" (p. 76), a legitimation for the importance of adult education. Adult educators need to collaborate with youth, learn from and with youth, and value the contributions of youth in order to move toward peaceful communities. Ross et al. (2010) argue, "youth and adults collaborate and learn from each other by moving toward horizontal group structures, sharing responsibilities, and building sufficient understanding of social and environmental contexts" (p. 197). The hierarchical social structures evident between youth and adults is problematic in the pursuit of peace. In this regard, DeKraai, Bulling, McLean, and Fletcher (2010) caution,

> The energy, passion, and creativity of youth often lead to unique solutions to problems in our society. However, youth and their adult partners are

situated in historical social constructions of youth as unskilled and incapable, in need of adult guidance in community change. In this paradigm, adults are the experts who take leadership and responsibility and thus hold the power in community and social change. This stance is especially evident for those youth who have traditionally been marginalized in our society. (p. 75)

Considering youth live in "an adult-controlled world," youth-adult collaborations and intergenerational learning and living are essential to building peace (Lindeman, 1937, as cited in Briton, 1996, p. 76). Thus, this research was oriented toward intergenerational learning by incorporating shared insights on violence transformation and strategies for building cultures of peace with both young adults and older adults engaged in peace work. The back and forth sharing of insights enabled diverse perspectives to be considered, valued, and critiqued. Future research where youth and older adults are engaged as participants together would further contribute to the development of methodological processes supporting adult-youth collaborative learning.

Engaging youth and youth adults in processes for social change, through role modeling, mentorship, and intergenerational learning must be valued as part of lifelong learning (Christens & Dolan, 2011). Adult-youth collaborations benefit youth, adult partners, and the community as a whole (Warner, Langlois, & Dumand, 2010). Adult-youth partnerships can challenge negative perceptions of youth and create supportive environments where the contributions of youth are valued (Warner, Langlois, & Dumand, 2010). More research is required to better understand the participation, engagement, and activism among youth in Canada (Lange & Chubb, 2009).

According to UNESCO (2002) fostering a *culture of peace* through educational frameworks involves developing curricula and programming "to promote the qualitative values, attitudes and behaviour inherent in a culture of peace; training for conflict prevention and resolution, dialogue, consensus-building and active non-violence" (p. 9). In relation to youth, constructions of enmity and the pursuit of a *culture of peace*, more research is required to better understand attitudes and behaviors in times of peace and war (Raviv, Oppenheimer, & Bar-Tal, 1999). More research is also required to understand the roles of youth in transforming conflict and violence (McEvoy-Levy, 2001). Youth need to be involved in identifying problems and creating methods for change in a way where participation is real and influential in the area of policy development and governance practices (Susskind, 2010; UNESCO, 2004). This is especially important considering youth leadership development has been shown to have an impact in the area of violence reduction and prevention

(Bickmore, 2011). In a Canadian study, Bickmore (2011) found that youth leadership and peer engagement in the area of conflict transformation are effective methods to challenge the normalization of violence within public schools. Additional research exploring youth leadership and peer engagement in community-based peace work will be a valuable contribution in this area.

1   Young Adult Participants: Demographics & Relationships

My understandings of violence and peace work are influenced by years of working in the area of youth engagement and leadership development. The youth I have had the pleasure to work with within schools and communities, have inspired me to continue the pursuit for a more peaceful world, where respectful relations are the core focus of our existence. The youth I have mentored and learned with have strengths, abilities, and resiliencies that are often unacknowledged and not valued in the wider society. I have learned a tremendous amount from youth who have continuously pushed me to consider alternative approaches to peacebuilding.

Ten Canadian young adults living in Nova Scotia, and volunteering for the Canadian Red Cross Even Wars Have Limits program, participated in this research process exploring how power influences the construction of enmity, and how learning opportunities and peace pedagogies can be created to challenge and transform enmity constructions. Even Wars Have Limits (EWHL) was a youth leadership development program where young adults (ages 18–30) developed education and activism skills while at the same time engaged other youth to become active global citizens. The EWHL volunteers participated in weekly three-hour meetings, learning both content (for example, impact and consequences of armed conflict) and skills (for example, advocacy, curriculum development, and public engagement) in relation to international humanitarian law and education based peace work. After many hours of training and collaborative learning, the EWHL youth leaders hosted community events such as workshops, symposiums, and film screenings focused on armed conflict and conflict transformation, as well as facilitating skills workshops in a variety of areas, including public speaking, how to lead social issues groups, and project planning. Working with youth who are already engaged as humanitarian educators, and who have had experiences teaching and learning with hundreds of youth in Nova Scotia, allowed for an opportunity to reflect on personal constructions of enmity, as well as on their teaching practices. Through this process, the experiences of the participants both as young adults and as humanitarian educators were valued.

Nine of the 10 youth were women; 8 were between 19–24 years of age (two were between 25–29); all participants identified their race as white; seven identified their ethnicity as Canadian, one as Canadian-Acadian, and two identified as Canadian plus additional ethnicities;[2] two identified as Christians, two as Atheists, two unsure, and four did not declare; two participants identified themselves as being from lower class, four from middle class, two from upper class, and two did not declare. Finally with regard to educational backgrounds, two had recently completed Bachelor of Arts degrees and were working in the community, four were currently studying international development (some with a dual major in other subject areas), one was in law, one in journalism, and two were studying social sciences at the graduate level (see Table 5.1). The demographic information described above was largely collected during our first focus group as we explored our multiple identities and worldviews. Throughout our time together we discussed the interrelationships between our identities, experiences and worldviews. Our collective focus on commonalities and differences enabled us to explore how enmity constructions may be impacted by our complex identities and experiences.

The young adult participants spent eight months learning together how power influences enmity constructions and how peace pedagogies can be created towards building cultures of peace. Their insights about the normalizations of violence provide an invaluable glimpse into the power mechanisms supporting violence. The lack of literature focusing on youth and young adults engaged in peace work outside of formal education structures is

TABLE 5.1   Youth participant [3] – demographics

	Race/Ethnicity	Gender	Age	Education	Class
Ziko	White/Canadian	Male	18–24	Undergrad	Middle
Opal	White/Acadian	Female	25–29	Undergrad – completed	Middle
Audrey	White/Canadian	Female	25–29	Graduate level	Upper
Isla	White/Canadian Plus	Female	18–24	Undergrad	Middle
Lily	White/Canadian	Female	18–24	Undergrad	Lower
Amya	White/Canadian	Female	18–24	Undergrad – completed	Middle
Crystal	White/Canadian	Female	18–24	Undergrad	Middle
Rachel	White/Canadian	Female	18–24	Graduate level	Middle
Kira	White/Canadian Plus	Female	18–24	Undergrad	Middle
Dexie	White/Canadian	Female	18–24	Undergrad	Upper

problematic if cultures of peace are to be built. Peacebuilding education that neglects the voices, perspectives and participation of youth fails to consider the everyday experiences of youth and the powers operating within youth cultures.

Recognizing that active engagement of youth is critical for societal transformation (ICRC, 2011; UNESCO, 2011), it is essential that we increase understandings of how young adults come to learn violence and the construction of an enemy, and furthermore how learning opportunities and pedagogies can be created to challenge enmity constructions. It is a complex exploration that requires an inter-subjective and transdisciplinary approach. In relation to this study, many gaps are evident in the literature: a lack of Canadian research exploring constructions of enmity and normalizations of violence, particularly with youth; a lack of focus on how power influences enmity constructions; a lack of literature considering the creation of learning spaces and transdisciplinary pedagogies to challenge violence in the pursuit of building peaceful communities (WHO, 2014); and a lack of literature looking into youth as social agents for change. The literature review also highlights our collective failure, particularly within the adult education field, to engage young adults in learning, teaching and facilitating peace processes. When youth and young adults are engaged in learning and teaching for peace, possibilities for conflict transformation may be realized towards more inclusive, peaceful communities.

Notes

1 The reference to 300,000 child soldiers engaged in armed conflicts has been a contested number due to the challenges of accessing data revealing the numbers of children engaged.
2 By sharing the specific countries referenced in relation to ethnicity, the anonymity the participants may be compromised.
3 Pseudonyms are used for the participants.

CHAPTER 6

Participatory, Critical and Collaborative Research *with* Youth

> If knowledge represents power, and we are committed to developing knowledge that generates social change and actions that improve life for people, it makes sense to involve those people and others who are intimately acquainted with the issues.
>
> KIRBY, GREAVES, & REID, *Experience Research Social Change: Methods beyond Mainstream* (2010, p. 30)

∴

The study utilized a collaborative and participatory methodology to center the perspectives and voices of 10 Canadian young adult[1] educators, who were actively engaged in teaching about conflict-related humanitarian issues as volunteers with the Canadian Red Cross. This qualitative research was situated in a critical paradigm where emphasis was placed on a critique of power relations and knowledge constructions (Merriam, 2009). A critical approach enabled a deep analysis of the power mechanisms involved in the construction of enmity (or the *dehumanized* other) and the maintenance of violence within the lives of the youth participants due to the underlying recognition that violence is shaped by societies and the relations of power within them (Francis, 2002).

Together, the young adult educators and I explicitly examined how power influences their constructions of an enemy, including their shared understandings and variations in perspectives on socialization processes. We also examined how peace processes may be created to challenge and transform these constructions. The purpose of this study was to gain insight into the socialized norms operating in the lives of Canadian young adults in relation to constructions of enmity and the normalizations of violence, in order to create learning opportunities for peaceful transformations. Learning *with* the youth participants was central to this research process.

1   Participatory and Collaborative Research – Inspirations from PAR

Participatory Action Research (PAR) is a process-oriented methodological approach that values and legitimizes people's knowledge by emphasizing "the use of knowledge as one of the major bases for power and control in our societies" (Tandon, 2002a, p. 206). The key ideas of PAR include a focus on inclusion, participation, dialogue, action, social change, and empowerment (Hall, 2002; Gaventy & Merrifield, 2002; Kirby, Greaves, & Reid, 2010). A particular emphasis is placed on education and action with the assumption that action, or learning by doing, produces a different kind of knowledge (Brown, 2002; Kirby, Greaves, & Reid, 2010; Tandon, 2002a). PAR is meant to be a collaborative learning process focused on engaging marginalized people and communities to create change and increase capacities for a more equitable life (Kincheloe, 2009; Gaventy & Merrifield, 2002; Kirby, Greaves, & Reid, 2010; Tandon, 2002a). For this research project our collaborative learning enabled us to focus on community social action while at the same time exploring opportunities to improve teaching practices among young adult educators who are engaged as community-based peacebuilding educators.

PAR aspires to "bottom-up knowledge systems" where the knowledge of people affected by the social issue being considered is strongly valued (Tandon, 2002d). Tandon (2002c) argues "the starting point for creating new knowledge is the existing knowledge of the people" (p. 44). Embraced within PAR is an appreciation for the agency and skills of the people affected/involved (Bryceson, Manicom, & Kassam, 2002). Participatory research embraces an intimate connection between the researcher(s), the participant-researchers, and the community, where dialogue and reflexivity are centered in knowledge formulation and validation (Bryceson, Manicom, & Kassam, 2002). PAR also creates spaces for new ideas and ways of knowing to emerge, particularly honouring the experiences and local knowledges of those engaged as participant-researchers (Fals-Borda & Rahman, 1991).

2   Participatory and Collaborative Methodologies *with* Youth

While youth are a heterogeneous population not typically categorized as marginalized as a whole, and recognized as having multiple identities, capacities, and lived experiences, the majority of youth in Canada do not have regular access to spaces (such as community, municipal, provincial, or federal) where political, educational, and justice-oriented policies are created, nor do they have systematic influence during discussions focused on violence prevention and peace promotion within communities. In this regard, it is important to acknowledge the exclusion experienced by most youth, in relation to adults, and the growing separation of children and youth from adult privileged activities, particularly formal leadership opportunities.

Collaborative methodologies offer a strong framework for working with youth and for considering the emphasis on valuing the knowledge and participation of those affected/involved (McGregor, 2010). McGregor (2010) suggests that we should reconstruct "the research paradigm to one in which youth are viewed as knowers of their world and experts in their own right, rather than 'unfit'" (p. 123), part of a deficit model that is so often predominant in education (Freire, 2003). As with any socially constructed group, the authenticity of the participatory engagement is of utmost importance with youth (McGregor, 2010). By engaging in a PAR-inspired methodology, opportunities arose to empower each other as collaborative researchers exploring social issues affecting youth for the purpose of creating change.

In an *honest* PAR methodology, the participants should own and lead the entire process, a practice which is constrained in academia. Inspired by the social justice and collaborative traditions of PAR, I endeavoured to conduct a democratic research process *with* the youth participants and not *for* them. These young Canadians engaged in an emergent critical exploration of how power influences enmity constructions, and the possibilities for creating learning spaces and pedagogies to challenge the normalization of violence, particularly the socialized norms of violence evident in the everyday lives of the youth participants. The perspectives of the youth participants were central to the research process and analysis. We continually navigated valuing our individual and collective knowledge(s), while at the same time, exploring and critiquing the origins of these knowledges. We also engaged in on-going critical reflections of power relations, both in terms of content and the context in which we learned together.

While the skeleton of the research process, including the selection of methods, was pre-determined as per academic requirements, there was opportunity for the participants to influence how each method was utilized and organized in the study. For instance, the youth participants identified the pertinent questions to consider when analyzing social constructions of enmity; they led the individual, informal dialogue, determining the important inclusions to share and selected the photo representations of enmity to discuss during our time together; they also selected the photos to share with the larger group for further examination; they contributed to shaping the key areas of focus for our group dialogue (during the individual, informal dialogues, each participant was invited to help shape the focus group agenda); they determined the final data sets to be analyzed; they led the data analysis, including determining how and when lessons shared by 6 professional informants[2] were incorporated; and they developed a process to further explore the problem of enmity constructions and possible strategies for change.

3 Methods: Pedagogical Processes

In congruence with the collaborative and participatory methodological framework, the research methods focused on critical reflection and dialogue, participation, shared learning, and social action. A multi-method approach enhanced opportunity for plurality of perspectives, participant engagement, and reflexivity. The data collection methods included: participant-generated photos, reflective journals, individual interviews, and participation in two focus groups. The methods chosen were intended to create space for individual critical reflection, group reflection and critical analysis, teamwork, opportunity for action, as well as flexibility and responsiveness to participant influence. The research took place in Halifax, Nova Scotia, Canada.

3.1 *Reflective Journaling*

To initiate the research process, we engaged in self-reflection about our assumptions, our identity(ies), our understandings of enmity, our understandings of power, and the interrelations between enmity and power. During our 8 months together, participants were invited to share journal entries if they so chose (journals were not collected to encourage uninhibited reflections). Some participants chose to read excerpts from their journals during one-on-one interviews with me, as well as during our two focus groups.

3.2 *Arts-Based: Participant-Generated Photography*

Each participant was given a disposable camera and invited to capture images representing enmity in their everyday lives, and how power influences these constructions. The participants were provided ethical guidelines from the Canadian Council for International Cooperation for the use of photography to protect the dignity of individuals captured in photos and to ensure a more ethical consideration for shared imagery (CCIC, 2008) (Appendix 1). Our discussions around ethical imagery provided an important framework to continue our focus on constructions of enmity, respectful relations, and the ethics of participatory methods.

3.3 Individual, Informal Dialogue – Youth Participants

I conducted 10 individual conversations/interviews[3] with the participants in October 2013 (Appendix 2). During our conversation, the participant-generated photos were analyzed as a tool to initiate discussion (Merriam, 2009). The dialogue took place in the form of an informal, conversational interview at a site selected by the participant in recognition of relational considerations (Chilisa, 2012) and issues of power (such as the researcher – researchee relationship) that need to be visible within a participatory process (Lee, 2012). The conversations took place in public spaces such as coffee shops, university cafeterias, libraries, and study rooms. All locations were bustling environments, frequented by young adults in our community, and part of the everyday living spaces for the participants. The interviews focused on the participants' experience reflecting on their visual representations of enmity and power. The interviews/discussions concluded with an invitation for the participants to develop questions and strategies for the focus groups. The participants also selected the photos they wished to share with the large group during the focus groups.

3.4 Interview Guide Approach – Professional Informants

In addition to the participatory engagement of youth, and keeping in line with my practice, and the practice within EWHL[4] encouraging mentorship and co-learning between youth and adults, I interviewed 6 adult *professional informants*[5] (PIs) who were experienced critical pedagogues in the areas of peace education, global education, humanitarian law education, peace building, peace keeping, and peace activism. The PIs were invited to share key insights and lessons learned from their rich and lengthy experiences working towards cultures of peace. Learning with experienced adults who support engagement and leadership development in youth-led social justice work, can add perspectives where both adults and youth learn from each other (Linds & Goulet, 2010). In this regard I served as a connector between the youth and the PIs. At no time were the identities of the youth participants and PIs known to each other.

I used an interview guide approach with the professional informants. Within an interview guide approach, general topics are pre-determined in an outline but the questions are specifically defined during the interview (Quinn Patton, 2002). This type of interview method was a little more prescriptive in comparison to the informal conversational style described for the youth, however, it allowed for more opportunity to compare responses from the interviewees (Quinn Patton, 2002).

3.5   Focus Groups

The final method within this research project involved participation in two focus groups. I facilitated a full day participatory focus group in November, 2013, and facilitated the final participatory focus group in March, 2014 to tie our final analyses together. During the first focus group, participants identified aims, goals, and community standards to create a safer space for dialogue. The participants engaged in a power analysis to critically analyze their learning and teaching about enmity and normalizations of violence, based on their individual work exploring enmity and power through journaling and photography,

The first focus group was organized using the principles of Open Space for Dialogue and Enquiry (OSDE). OSDE uses a multi-step critical pedagogical process. Firstly, a stimulus is used to initiate critical thinking (Andreotti, 2011). In this case, the photos and data generated from the individual dialogues were used as the stimuli. Secondly, reflexive questions are used to encourage consideration of individual perspectives (Andreotti, 2011). The reflexive questions utilized were generated by the participants during our initial individual interviews. For example, questions included: "how does our worldview influence our understanding of an enemy?"; "how do our experiences influence how we teach others?"; "how does our formal school experience influence how we learn about conflict?" Following the use of reflexive questions, dialogue is encouraged to identify diverse perspectives and explore the origins of knowledge construction and power (Andreotti, 2011). During this phase of the group dialogue we specifically utilized Giroux's (1993) *pedagogy of representation*. We explored how representations of enmity are constructed; who benefits from the representations of enmity we were exploring; where the representations of enmity fit both politically and ethically; and how ideology and power influence representations of enmity (Giroux, 1993). We also used Gaventa's (2006) *Power Cube* to explore forms, spaces, and levels of power. We used the *Power Cube* to frame deeper questions about hidden and invisible power, such as explicit questions about ideological social conditioning. Questions ranged from exploring what power meant to each participant, how they see power operating in their lives, and how different forms of power influence representations of enmity.

The final phases of the OSDE process includes an exploration of strategies for action and collective responsibility (Andreotti, 2011). Participants were encouraged to critically analyze how power influences their enmity constructions, their teaching and learning about enmity and violence/peace, as well as possible collective actions to incorporate these learnings into their everyday lives and community-based activism. The focus group concluded by considering strategies for change, with a reflection on the learning (Andreotti, 2011). The youth participants discussed how an upcoming conference they were organizing with high school youth could be re-envisioned for effective and sustainable social change. They also discussed how EWHL curriculum materials could be enhanced to encourage long-term, critical, and collaborative movements for peace.

4 Community Standards and Participation Processes

Participation, voice, respect, and safe spaces were central themes in how we engaged in this research project. As a learning community, we developed many guidelines or community standards to help maintain certain ethics of engagement throughout our eight months together. From the beginning conversations around ethical imagery (Appendix 1), to our continual dialogue about confidentiality (especially given our group learning), to our development of community standards (which we created together, all received copies of and physically posted during our group gatherings) (Appendix 3), significant energy was expended towards building safer learning spaces where diverse voices and experiences were valued. Our community standards outlined the group *rules,* including the importance of using respectful language, agreeing to disagree, that all knowledge is partial, and we all have knowledge. One participant discussed our community standards and participatory process in an evaluation, stating:

> Overall, very good project with great engaging activities. Very inclusive environment. I felt welcome and safe to talk. Very happy we were moving around and engaging with one another. Did not feel pressured at any point to make, or abstain from making any comments.

By understanding the expectations of the participants, as individuals and as a group, we were able to adjust the focus or activity to ensure our expectations, experiences, and fears/concerns remained part of our conversations and processes.

5 PAR-Inspired Data Analysis

Veneklasen and Miller (2002) describe their work on power theories as a quilt kit, which includes tools and sample patterns to support the creation of a quilt, but does not prescribe a set pattern to follow. Our analysis process incorporated certain 'tools' and 'patterns', however, the process was emergent as the participants were central in shaping our approach. Furthermore, as in qualitative research generally, the data analysis was a simultaneous process with data collection (Creswell, 1994; Merriam, 2009; Wilson, 2008).

After individual processes for critical self-reflection in relation to exploring constructions of enmity (i.e. photo-taking, journaling, and individual interviews), our group came together to begin a collective dialogue and analysis of shared and divergent understandings of power and violence. Our collaborative learning was fundamental to our research process. Our collaborative learning also involved bringing additional voices and lenses to our conversation by including the key messages and lessons learned from the professional informants. The youth participants expressed great interest in the opportunity to learn together. For instance, in advance of our group discussion, Amya shared "I like hearing other people's opinions ... I am just excited for the conversation."

Mulit-level analyses were completed: (1) by the youth participants and I collaboratively exploring enmity constructions based on the participant-generated photos, our one-on-one interviews, and my field notes/journal; (2) I completed a systematic coding of the professional informant (PI) interviews to explore the range and variations in PIs' understandings of enmity constructions, youth as peace builders, and teaching and learning peaceful processes; (3) we compared and contrasted how participants represented enmity and power, as well as processes for teaching and learning peaceful processes. Following each group analysis, the summary of the discussions and conclusions were shared with the participants to ensure the essence and intended meanings were properly conveyed. The final analysis was written and shared with the participants via e-mail to ensure the conclusions reflect the participants' contributions and understandings.

6 Methodological Insights

Using a critical, collaborative and PAR-inspired methodology was complex, challenging, and required a high level of reflexivity, honesty, and openness to change. There were challenges and limitations, however, this methodological approach enabled spaces for co-learning to occur throughout the research process, for critical conversations stemming from diverse perspectives to take place in *safer* spaces, and for our shared critical examination of enmity constructions and normalizations of violence to develop in-depth. Our use of multiple methods allowed the participants to connect and consider how enmity constructions develop in their everyday lives and in multiple spaces. Our methodological approach has resulted in significant contributions to understanding and challenging violence, and toward building peaceful communities together. The following chapters capture our shared learnings, our collaborative analyses, as well as my overall analysis of the research study.

Notes

1. Again, I refer to the participants as youth and young adults interchangeably given the participants were between the ages of 19–25.
2. Six professional informants (PI) were selected via purposeful sampling from my professional network as a humanitarian educator with the Canadian Red Cross. Each PI was selected based on a minimum of twenty years of professional practice in one or more of the following areas: peace education, global education, humanitarian law education, peace building, peace keeping and peace activism. The PIs were from diverse geographic regions (Halifax to Vancouver). The PIs were included in this research project to provide reflection and share lessons learned from their extensive practice in peace work. Four of the professional informants (PIs) were women and two were men; all well established in their respective careers (3 were retired but still working in their fields). The diversity of experiences were a conscious part of the selection process to allow for diverse perspectives to be shared with the youth participants.
3. Throughout the research process I use the terms interview and conversation interchangeably in relation to the conversational/interviews between the youth and I.
4. Again, EWHL was the Even Wars Have Limits youth leadership development program of the Canadian Red Cross.
5. Together with the youth participants we decided to change the title from 'key informant' to professional informant for two reasons: to honour the experiences shared by the professional contributors; but most importantly, to reserve the title of 'key informant' for the youth participants themselves.

CHAPTER 7

Constructions of Enmity: Perspectives from Youth

> Along the way of life, someone must have sense enough and morality enough to cut off the chain of hate and evil.
> MARTIN LUTHER KING JR.

∴

Violence interpenetrates our lives in multiple ways and is deeply embedded within language, behavior, and symbols (for example, street names and statutes). Popular culture, family and friends, cultural contexts, and formal schooling all contribute to how we come to understand violence and how we dehumanize *others* (Hakvoort & Oppenheimer, 1999; Shultz, 2012). These constructions of violence are temporally, spatially and culturally informed. Through our explicit and critical analysis exploring how enmity is constructed, the young adult participants revealed hidden and invisible spaces where violence is maintained and nurtured, particularly in youth cultures. Our findings expose a societal normalization of violence and the possibilities within critical adult education to expose how power operates to maintain violence. By collaboratively engaging in peace research with youth, and by explicitly exploring hidden and invisible forms of power as a central component of violence, conflict transformations led by youth, become imaginable.

In this chapter, I share the perspectives of youth participants exploring constructions of enmity and how our relations and the context of our research promoted respect for diverse perspectives. I discuss the processes we created to enable safer spaces for controversial conversations and our strengths and failings in this regard. Finally, I explore the complimentary and contradictory perspectives as shared and organized by the youth.

1   Constructions of Enmity

Participants were invited to capture representations of *Enemy* in their everyday lives using disposable cameras and were encouraged to capture reflections in the journals provided as a strategy supporting critical reflection. After a two-week period, the youth participated in an individual, informal/conversational style interview with me, describing the process of locating representations of enmity and their reflections on the power influences involved in these constructions. All participants described an awakening process, or a new level of *critical consciousness* (Freire, 1970), during the photography activity, highlighting how the intentional focus on locating relations, spaces or incidents of enmity revealed elements of violence in their everyday lives they had not noticed before. Lily stated she "was surprised by how much there is [enemy constructions] that I hadn't realized" and further added "studying about conflict [in International Development courses] made me more aware of it in general, but even just looking for it here, I found things that I didn't realize that were present." Lily also described how she began to recognize relations of power, dominance, and feelings of powerlessness after participating in the photography activity. She stated

> I never really thought about ... power and conflict or fighting and competition and stuff. We don't think about it because we grew up in an environment where like sports – it's all about the competition, yeah its totally the norm and I never thought about how people use that, not even meaning to, generating power over people. It's kind of scary.

Lily's reflection highlights the role of critical pedagogy and critical adult education to challenge our common sense views of violence, to move toward disrupting violence. Lily's comments also speak to the hidden and invisible forms of power that maintain an internalized acceptance of violence as a normal aspect of our society.

The photos captured and shared by the participants touched on multiple elements within our society related to violence and learned dehumanization processes, including patriarchy, systems of exclusion, tensions between differing interests, and the impact of competition and rivalry. The following discussion presents the youths' analysis of how enmity is constructed based on the participant generated images[1] and our informal conversational interviews and explores the range and variation of the youth's understanding of constructions of enmity.

1.1   *Finding #1: Identity(ies) as Different – Deficient*

"Everyone has a lens to view the world. And how powerful that is. And we make decisions without ever reflecting back on where this decision came from" (Audrey). Audrey's reflections about enmity constructions emphasized how our own identities influence how we see the identity(ies) of others. For Audrey, there is a lack of criticality applied in our everyday actions and a failure to critically reflect on our assumptions, leading to complicity in hegemonic ideologies as a result. In this regard, Dexi argues, "first off, we have to have a sense of who we are and secondly, we have to have a sense of who we are working with" in order to better understand violence and possibilities for peace. Thus, to understand how enmity is constructed we have to look at ourselves first.

While the photos represented diverse interpretations of enmity, the majority of the participants took a selfie[2] to discuss enmity constructions and to demonstrate how their complex identities and worldviews influence their understandings. Crystal shared a selfie with the caption "I am my own enemy – but why? Change your perception of yourself." Crystal explored internal tensions around identity(ies) and described why critical self-reflections are an important place to begin. Crystal's observation addresses the subjectivity(ies) of identity and connects with Barker's (2008) notion of performativity, the ability to perform an identity. Delving into how performativity influences the construction of identity, are important aspects to study in the deconstruction of enmity.

Many participants shared photos of themselves, including blurry photos or photos of a mirror image to discuss where and how beliefs (i.e. ideologies) are learned. As represented in the image of the foggy mirror below (see Figure 7.1), the youth explored how identities of self are constructed and the importance of reflecting on the self in relation to other and/or we to better understand ourselves and *othering*. Focusing on the self, and the self in structural productions, is an approach argued by Spivak (1990) in order to challenge processes of *othering*.

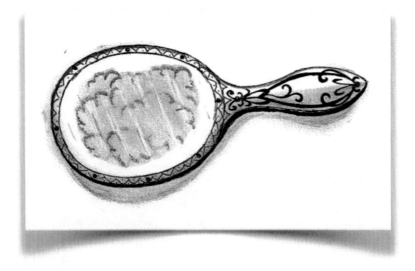

FIGURE 7.1   Image representing multiple 'selfies' and the complexity of identity(ies)

Amya argued that our identities and our idea of an enemy "comes from personal lived experience," complicated by familial and community influences but perhaps, most significantly influenced by the identity(ies) each person connects to, or rejects. In this regard, Audrey shared a photo of a Bible with the caption "a key part of my worldview," and discussed how our spiritual beliefs (including the lack of) influence how we see ourselves and others. Francis (2002) argues spirituality and religion are important aspects of identity, a reality often forgot in the increasingly secularized environments in the West. Audrey's example highlights the importance of naming and understanding our ontological frameworks, particularly in contexts where difference in identity (perceived or real), result in difference as deficient.

1.2   Finding #2: Disengaged Citizenship

Many of the photos captured the notion of *disengaged citizenship* as an integral element in the constructions of violence and enmity. Lily discussed the impact of our "individualistic focus" and Ziko added that a focus on the self, removes "the ability to connect with people." To illustrate *disengaged citizenship*, Isla shared a photo of a spilled garbage can (see Figure 7.2) and utilized the caption: "no one willing to take responsibility" to describe a process leading toward "disengaged citizenship" and "apathy." Isla described watching person after person walking past the spilled garbage can as a symbol of disconnected people and our inability to share responsibility or see how our lives are interconnected.

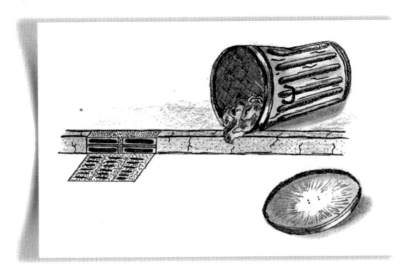

FIGURE 7.2   "No one willing to take responsibility. Disengaged citizenship" – Isla

Similarly, Lily suggested our apathy towards each other is

> because society is now very individualistic and it's all about being an independent person. Whereas like in the past, it was more about family, or collective oriented. But now it's all about being your own person. You are an individual person doing your own thing and accomplishing what you want to accomplish, which makes people a little more defensive or aggressive in sort of maintaining their own, like independence and dominance, which I guess, yeah it causes competition rather than working together.

Discussions about disconnected citizenship focused on both local and international contexts. Crystal created a sign displaying "Humanitarian aid and the lack of global citizenship" as a representation of a global disconnect. Crystal's caption read "development depression – how can we overcome? We have a responsibility to others." Similar to Isla's focus on disengagement, Crystal described how our ability to create enmity is impacted by our global detachment, which is fuelled by globalization where goods and services trump equitable relations. Further to this, Crystal suggested "the enemy is that people don't care enough if it is not right in front of our face and if it is not happening to them." The discussions with the youth participants around disengagement connects to Thayer-Bacon's work (2003), exploring relational epistemologies and the de-centering of relations from our ways of knowing and learning.

The youth described multiple relational contexts including: personal experience, familial and community influences, which contribute to understandings of self and our ability to associate (or not) with *others*. Kira discussed how formal education systems contribute to a distinguishing of self and other when there is "subtle tweaking … certain groups or certain people get portrayed more negatively then perhaps they would otherwise. Or stories are told differently … They are left out, despite something that happened they give it a lot more prominence." In this regard, Kira is emulating an example of Giroux's *pedagogy of representation,* and highlighting the consequences of our failure to question and challenge how history, stories and representations are created and shared. Kira described the opportunities within formal education to build inclusive communities, but claimed her school experience maintained an *us* versus *them* approach to the study of historical conflict.

The youth also described a continuum of identity constructions stemming from self to other and then from other to enemy. The progression from other to enemy was described by Ziko as a process of "dehumanizing them [enemy] and attributing everything negative and nothing positive." Ziko recounted situations of armed conflict to further his argument and shared a photo of bullets and shrapnel with the caption: "Separating. Never seeing those considered the enemies allows them to be dehumanized. Sometimes the only interaction in a conflict is via a weapon." In the context of armed violence, Ziko discussed the physical space that can occur between *self* and *other* and how in the midst of conflict, spatial location can contribute to the dehumanization processes. Ziko emphasized that an enemy is often someone you have no relationship with, again, speaking to the lack of embodiment of relational ways of knowing (conscious or unconscious).

In contrast to *disengaged citizenship*, other participants described collective citizenship and opportunities for learning constructions of love and friendship. Audrey shared a photo of a group of people in church hugging and praying together and included the following caption: "families and friends praying together. Support within community. Collective identity." Audrey described how solidarity can lead to constructions of togetherness and connection as opposed to enmity. Likewise, Kira described the practice of collective citizenship as "connectedness to society or a broader group" and explored possibilities for peace, together. Both Audrey and Kira described and appreciated difference within community or collective citizenship, while sharing a common vision of solidarity: respect for self, other, and we. Freire (1970) also describes solidarity as being integral to collective social action and passionately urged for love to be central in our everyday actions.

Opal similarly discussed how solidarity and group collective action can challenge constructions of enmity. Opal chose a photo of a community sign: "Raymond Taavel healing garden"[3] while discussing the process of community solidarity and the importance of collective healing when surviving the impacts of violence. Opal shared how the community "chose peace" in their healing journey instead of constructing the perpetrator of this violent act as an enemy. She described how the community navigated their anger and grief with a conscious decision to refrain from dehumanizing persons with mental health diseases and disorders, despite media and public discourse linking mental health and violence. Riordon (2011) argues that violent narratives are the dominant story stemming from conflict, a claim she makes while uncovering countless untold stories of solidarity in Israel and Palestine. Riordon (2011) calls for collecting and sharing cooperative and solidarity narratives as a method to challenge normalizations of violence.

1.3   Finding #3: Systems of Exclusion

Building on the discussion of disconnected people and communities, many participants described systems of exclusion as enabling and promoting dehumanized constructions of other. The participants described non-inclusive environments, labeling and stereotyping, access and equity issues, as well as barriers and restrictions to participation, as practices leading toward and sustaining constructions of enmity.

Dexie, Isla, Lily and Rachel explored patriarchy and masculinity as being rooted within constructions of enmity and as an explicit system of exclusion. Isla shared a photo of a sign: "CAUTION!! Men Working in Lobby" and expressed her concern about the "blatant inequality and non-inclusive environments" and how these pervasive, yet embedded symbols and signs, contribute to our constructions of the negative other. Isla stated, "We've gotten so used to seeing these signs that we don't even question it or say anything about it but it made me angry." Dexie also viewed patriarchy as a quintessential element in the manifestation of enmity, focusing her reflections on the global narrative of violence and patriarchy, using human trafficking and the gendered realities in forced migration as an example. The examples above speak to Galtung's (1996) assertion that "patriarchy, like any other deeply violent social formation (such as criminal subcultures and military structures), combines direct, structural, and cultural violence in a vicious triangle" (p. 40). Related to Isla and Dexie's examples, Galtung (1996) has long argued violence is complex but largely rests within and among men.

Rachel also explored patriarchy, but in the context of her own identity and the pressure to "adhere to gender roles, especially at work." She shared a photo of make-up to represent the identity she feels is assigned to her, or expected of her, in order to be accepted professionally (see Figure 7.3). Rachel discussed how our physical appearance is integral to inclusion or exclusion and described the interconnections between sexism and racism, stating: "on the appearance factor, it really defines how you are allowed to even interact. If you are a certain

FIGURE 7.3   "Adhering to gender roles, especially at work." – Rachel

race, certain things are expected, or allowed or excused just based on how you look." In our discussion, Rachel shared many personal examples of how racism and sexism interpenetrate identities of self and other and can lead to a process supporting the dehumanized other.

Beyond patriarchy Ziko suggested that systems of exclusion involve framing others as "so different and our lifestyles are incompatible and therefore we must defend ourselves, which kind of creates that idea of an enemy." Here Ziko explored how our disassociations and disconnections can manifest into accepted and embodied differences, leading to actions and practices that maintain the other as less than ourselves and as a threat to our way of being. Guo (2009) describes this process as the creation of a deficient other. Similarly, Opal suggested "an enemy is anyone who is going to get in the way of their goals ... so they can consider anyone who is against them a bad guy." In this regard, Frantzi (2004) argues that "alienation and dehumanization appear when people cannot see this unity in their every thought and action, but set the dualism of 'I-You', 'Us-Them'" (p. 1).

Several youth discussed how framing others within a binary of being against or with us, results in the escalation of exclusion and increased security measures. For example, Isla shared a photo of a sign indicating that customers of a convenience store, customers who are largely youth, must press a buzzer to enter the store. She questioned the grounds in which staff in the store allowed or disallowed potential customers and wondered if the location of the store was different (i.e. not in proximity to a university or youth) if the practice would be different. Isla suggested this example identified a physical exclusion, based on visible identities, or perceived identities, and the "creation of systems to keep certain groups out or un-included." In relation to securitization and exclusions within migration, Kira shared "not everyone is welcome. Not everyone is protected in the same way." Kira identified the development of migration rules based on countries of origin, as an example of non-inclusive and binary focused policies in practice. Isla's and Kira's examples of enmity touch on Tcherepashenets (2011) explorations of *othering* being infused with fear, and the increasing securitization structures stemming from the impact of globalization.

1.4 *Finding #4: Normalizations of Violence*

The youth participants described how the photography activity facilitated the development or the enhancement of an explicit lens for seeing normalizations of violence in their everyday lives. The participants illustrated many examples from recreation (ex., video games), to local buildings (ex., competing businesses), to emerging spaces (ex., social media) where violence is an accepted normal. Lily described how "subliminal violence" – or *cultural violence*, creeps into our lives and norms often unseen and typically unchallenged, arguing: "there is not enough attention paid to that."

The participants discussed the association of youth culture and violence, both challenging and supporting this association in the images shared. Lily discussed the interrelations between masculinity and violence, sharing a photo of a young man on a porch "giving the middle finger" with the caption "flipping off the other, sort of a 'you suck' mentality." For Lily, this image represented an accepted norm of violence among young men. Lily also shared a photo of her roommate's bedroom, which was filled with "war paraphernalia," including guns. She described watching her male roommates laughing, while playing video games where their characters were punching and kicking women. Reflecting on this experience, Lily stated

> this pissed me off so much...this wasn't even part of the plot of the video game ... and when I say "it's not funny" they get all defensive and say "I don't know why you are so sensitive it was all a joke"... I don't find it funny, but it's ingrained in their head ... it's a joke to them.

She discussed how her male roommates' "fascination with war and means of war" were problematic and she questioned whether this interest in armed violence contributed to a desensitization of the impact of violence on people and communities. In contrast to Lily's discussion about war play and violence, Ziko suggested that as educators "we need to focus on what's real and what's fun and playful." For Ziko, gaming and war-related paraphernalia did not lead to heightened levels of violent constructs or behavior, and revealed that he frequently engaged in "war play" for recreation, fully capable of distinguishing between the two.

Several participants described how physical spaces, such as buildings, can represent deep rooted, and often unchallenged violence. Opal discussed how a street in her community named after Lieutenant General Cornwallis,[4] a British officer who once heralded as a founder of Halifax, serves as a symbol to validate violence, particularly towards Aboriginal persons. She explained how historical influences and the continued impact of colonialism thrives in physical spaces and suggested that we need to challenge these elements of structural and cultural violence to prevent further manifestations of enmity constructions. Opal addressed the deep-rooted nature of violence, particularly of colonization, as an example of how enmity is built within relations including our interactions in physical spaces. Constructions of the dehumanized *other* stem from multiple interpenetrating elements of our lives and Opal's call for critique of violent symbols in our everyday environments, emulates the need for an enhanced *critical consciousness* (Freire, 1970) and highlights the opportunity for critical pedagogy as an educational strategy for engaging peace work.

In connection to Opal's discussion about the legacy of colonialism and the violence embedded within physical spaces and symbols, Isla shared a photo of a cartoon posted on a mail box depicting "a picture of Jewish man." The cartoon was composed in a derogatory manner with dress, hair and facial features drawn in exaggerated form. Isla described how labels and perpetuated stereotypes exist in our physical environment and how we regularly engage (consciously or unconsciously) with these representations of violence. She wondered why there was no effort to remove this symbol from a public space and how long this image remained posted. Similarly, Opal shared a photo of a building covered in graffiti, which included the question "what is the history of this building?" (see Figure 7.4). She wondered what took place in this building, what was being concealed from the community, who wrote the question, and why she had not noticed the inscription before.

In addition to physical spaces, social media was explored by multiple participants as an alternative site where violence is normalized yet where solidarity can also be nurtured. Crystal suggested that social media "is being used negatively to create that enemy culture." She described how anonymity enables and facilitates a higher degree of violence due to the lack of accountability, responsibility, or relations evident in actions taken. She further stated "social media is our enemy ... especially for younger generations, it's very much a way to target others and it's not creating a culture of sensitivity, which I think is important. So in a way, it is working against us [youth]." In relation to social media, Lily shared a screen shot of

FIGURE 7.4   "What is the history of this building?" – Opal

Facebook and discussed social media as a space for normalizing violence, describing how her roommates often engage in conflict via Facebook. For Lily, the lack of physical proximity associated with the use of social media, contributes to escalations of conflict and "passive aggressive othering." She shared "I don't see a lot of physical conflict in everyday experiences, but I see a lot of passive aggression through Facebook."

Conversely, Crystal, Lily, and Dexie discussed opportunities for peace building through social media. All three participants distinguished the space and the use of the space as being a key consideration when exploring peace and violence. Crystal shared a photo of her laptop and cell phone (see Figure 7.5) to discuss the dual role of technology generally, and social media specifically, in relation to normalizations of violence and the possibilities for nurturing solidarity. Lily shared a screen shot of a Facebook group rallying together to advocate against fracking and explored how "using social media to unify ... and raise awareness" can lead to collective action. Dexie described how the use of social media to connect with activists in other regions and countries, enables her to feel united to a larger cause and connected to people who also work towards transforming violence. Instead of viewing social media as a negative or positive space, Ziko argued that social media and technology are "just another way of socializing," and like other spaces where people connect, there are both opportunities and risks associated.

FIGURE 7.5   "Misuse of social media – why does it have to be that way?" – Crystal

1.5   *Finding #5: Competition and Rivalry*

Connected to normalizations of violence, many participants discussed the role of competition and rivalry in the construction of enmity. Opal described two scenarios where corporate interests and development issues clashed. In the first example, she shared a photo of graffiti located on a community building which was being re-considered for corporate purposes. The graffiti stated "Don't be pushed out." Opal described the polar positions being argued by those engaged (i.e. the corporation and the community organization currently using the space) and wondered whether the needs of both parties could be met through a respectful, community building process. In another example, Opal shared a photo of a clay art project wrapped around a telephone poll in the most corporate region of Halifax. For her, the location of the art project demonstrated competing interests.

Related to Opal's discussion about competition, Ziko shared a photo of coins to discuss how conflict and the creation of an enemy can be fuelled by resources. Ziko stated, "People will attack each other or dehumanize each other for certain economic benefits." Rachel also discussed the role of competition over resources as a source of enmity constructions, stating, "Money is such a dominating force. Sometimes it can be a societal enemy."

Lily and Amya also explored competition as an impetus for dehumanization processes. Lily described an on-going conflict between two corner stores located on adjacent corners. She captioned a photo of the stores with "competitive businesses trying to outdo the other one. Use of the words 'best,' 'original,' etc." Lily described how residents watch the conflict unfold daily as store signs boasting the uniqueness and the superiority of the respective store are posted regularly. Similar to the competing corner store example, Amya shared a photo of a grocery store sign as a representation of the *enemy*. She described that growing up, a family member worked at a grocery chain, so for Amya, the corporate competitor was the enemy. In relation to competition and violence, Francis (2002) argues "although issues of identity – tribe, nationality, ethnicity, religion – have been presented as the cause of so many recent wars, strategic interests and economic factors often play a fundamental role" (p. 4).

Finally, Lily discussed the role of media in fuelling violence through the lens of competition and rivalry. She shared a photo of a TV screen shot of the show The Voice[5] as an example. The photo illustrated a boxing style stage with competitor A vs. competitor B written across the screen (see Figure 7.6). The show, which claims to assess singing talent objectively due to the judges' inability to see the contestants when they perform, has competition embedded from beginning to end. Lily described the terms used in the show, for example the ring to refer to the stage, and battle rounds to specify when two singers compete for the judges. Lily recounted the joy this show brought to her and her roommates until the photography activity resulted in her seeing "subliminal violence" ingrained in a TV show she would have previously described as non-violent. Again, the photos and representations shared indicate opportunities

FIGURE 7.6   "Even TV shows are designed on the enemy. Battle rounds, __ vs. __, and the stage set is set up like a boxing ring." – Lily

for critical pedagogical approaches to challenge unexamined assumptions. The youth argue for the development of a *critical consciousness* (Freire, 1970) to elevate our critical reflections and create opportunities for social transformation.

By using photography as an opportunity to deeply reflect on the violence in their everyday lives, the youth participants revealed commonalities and differences in understandings of enmity constructions and the spaces and relations where dehumanized constructions of other may be fostered. The youth acknowledged how their identity(ies) influenced the images they captured. For example, Audrey referenced her faith as a key influencing factor, while Ziko discussed his experience in armed conflict as a lens, which shapes his understandings of enmity constructions.

2   Looking back, Learning together, Moving ahead: Key Insights from Professional Informants

To understand the role of the professional informants (PIs) in this study, it is important to explain the interactions between the PIs and the youth participants. I interviewed the six PIs (one to two hours each), had the interviews transcribed, shared the transcriptions with the PIs for feedback and editing, coded the transcripts and shared key themes and key learnings as identified by the PIs with the youth participants. During the focus groups, the youth had access to this data (key themes) as well as quotes[6] from the PIs for use at any time and in a manner that they deemed appropriate. The data generated by the PIs was regularly referred to and considered in our discussions and critical reflections. The identities of the PIs were not shared with the youth.

The following section highlights the reflections of the PIs in relation to enmity constructions, including the similarities and differences shared.

2.1 *Constructions of Enmity – Professional Informant Perspectives*

Overwhelmingly, the PIs discussed the role of socialization in the normalization of violence. Socialization processes within the home, community, school (including the influence of curricula), and as a result of interactions with media were widely discussed as were the evolving nature of these internalization processes. Wenona[7] illustrated multiple sites and social influences in constructions of self, other and we, and generally described these influences as being contained in "the narratives that people get access to and find themselves immersed in, both in their families and communities, and in their school curriculum, formal and hidden and overt school curricula texts." In relation to socialization of enmity, Mei described how people "get to that incrementally because they learn it within the family, they learn it within their social circle." Similarly, Chester shared

> our children are taught to be suspicious of people who are different than they are, and to hate them and in fact, we are demonizing people who are not like us from an early age. So these values are socialized and it manifests itself throughout the life of an individual from childhood to adolescence to adulthood.

Juliana discussed "how we have made this process of creating the evil other. We have such a long history of it ... there has been this process of creating borders between people in order to strengthen a particular identity." Juliana further argued that our focus on "creating boundaries" and "historical cultural categories" leads to the development of a "deficient enemy" which is "cloaked in this legitimacy." The legitimacy of the dehumanized other is a main element of Galtung's (1996) version of cultural violence. According to Galtung (1996), cultural violence includes the components of culture such as religion, language, and science, which are used to legitimize violence. In this regard, Wenona discussed the role of symbols in legitimizing violence and referenced the work of Marc Howard Ross (2000) who argues that symbols and rituals can contain deep-rooted cultural violence. Cultural violence and the legitimacy afforded to enmity constructions was taken up by the professional informants in the aforementioned examples, and complements the youths' assertion that people are socialized to focus on identities as different or deficient.

In addition to the legitimation of violence as discussed above, Juliana attributed the construction of enmity with a dissociative process, sharing:

> we create stories and situations and images about this enemy, this person or people who are enemies. And then in such a way that they become unreachable in terms of relationship, that somehow they are so different that it would not be possible to recognize our own humanity in them, or theirs in us.

Mei also discussed the impact of decreasing connections among people, asking: "how do we get to the place of other rather than we? ... it's around [the lack of] identifying with the person ... or focusing on difference versus sameness." Ning described this process as well, arguing the "lack of empathy about other living conditions and other human experiences ... prevents us from empathizing with people." Chester described this process of disassociation in the context of armed conflict:

> when you think of someone as sub-human it is much easier to be brutal in confrontation with them. Because ordinary people do not go around killing or hurting people, it's so contrary to human nature, I think, and yet if you can demonize your target as someone who is less than human it is easier to unleash social discipline and do things that you wouldn't normally do.

Disassociation enables us to remove ourselves from fault, and blame those most directly affected by violence. Juliana summarized this process, stating:

> you know, we can say, your end of the boat is sinking, that somehow poverty is a problem of the poor, and violence is a problem of the child who's acted out and destroyed something ... whatever, somehow we assign that as being a problem somewhere outside of us ... the process of, um, of this separation and then to apply the idea of evil to them gets us to the enemy, right?

Our ability to assign blame and remove ourselves from culpability is an intentional element of the legitimation of the *deficient other* (Guo, 2009). In the examples provided, Mei, Chester, and Juliana, discussed the in-depth, systemic and embedded nature of cultural violence from everyday interactions to international armed conflict. This focus on disassociation connects to the youth's description of disengaged citizenship and systems of exclusion. Processes of disassociation are important areas for critique, particularly when dissociated remedies for conflict are often privileged (i.e. separating parties to a conflict). According to Galtung (1996), only negative peace is addressed and opportunities for creative conflict transformation are lost in peace processes that centre disassociation.

Media, social media and popular culture were also discussed at length in relation to enmity constructions and emerging socialization processes. Juliana stated "[popular culture] says that it's legitimate to have enemies, to be violent to address relationships through violence." Tarra spoke about the role of popular culture and media in identity constructions and argued: "the age of technology has interfered so dramatically with any kind of social interaction and I don't see that about to change any time soon." Likewise, Chester critiqued the practice of modern journalism, the role journalists play in creating the dehumanized other, and the public's interaction with media, stating "very few journalists provide the analysis that should go behind the story. It's just all sound bites, and clips and headlines." Chester further added that it is important to recognize "we are operating in an information vacuum at all times ... there is always information deficit." Galtung (2002) also described the detrimental role of journalism in relation to violence, arguing journalists predominantly focus on violence instead of the conflict, and fail to convey the complexity of the conflict. In this regard, the media have the ability to construct violence with certain images (Huq, 2002). Furthermore, public relation campaigns exercised through the media can "not only demonize the opponents; they also sanitize the allies" (Brand-Jacobsen, 2002, p. 33). Positive (allies) and negative (enemies) narrative constructions were also flagged by the youth participants as integral elements contributing to and normalizing the constructions of enmity.

In the examples above, Juliana, Tarra, and Chester raise important considerations for the role of critical pedagogy in teaching and learning critical media literacies. Giroux (1996) maintains "progressive educators must consider how the interface of cultural studies and critical pedagogy might be analyzed to create the conditions for social agency and institutional change among diverse sectors of youth" (p. 32). Recognizing the youth participants' focus on media, particularly social media, as sites for both the normalization of violence and building solidarity, a merging of cultural studies and critical pedagogy offers an important inter-disciplinary approach to exploring enmity constructions with youth.

Further to discussions about disassociation and lack of connections, within communities and via social media, Tarra highlighted the changing role of communities in the lives of youth and the shrinking spaces for intergenerational learning and living. Tarra remembered how the "village was alive and well" in her community during her youth and added: "the school is the only village left in the lives of most children." Thayer-Bacon (1999) argues "schools are called on to fill a gap in teaching morality that families and churches traditionally filled" (p. 140); and yet, schools are increasingly enacting surveillance measures to respond to conflict as opposed to engaging in peacebuilding (Bickmore, 2006). Lack of connections to and within community, particularly lack of elder support and intergenerational relations, are changing the socialization experiences of youth (Winfield, 1999) and according to Tarra, enabling violence. This discussion on the changing nature of community and interpersonal relations, connects to the youths' concern about disengaged citizenship and the increasing individualized society.

The professional informants (PIs) largely shared a focus on socialization processes as significant root causes of normalizations of violence, or the constructions of enmity. In addition to the examples provided, the PIs also shared other influences. For example, Chester discussed criminality or aspirations for economic gain and Wenona discussed power and control as a contributing factor in the construction of enmity. These examples are related to the youths' explorations of competition and rivalry as key root causes in the construction of dehumanized other.

Furthermore, Chester specified the lack of leadership or consequences for violent behaviour as important factors for increasing violent actions. Mei and Wenona highlighted the impact of individual experiences, psychological experiences, including fearful experiences, as influencing factors in dehumanization processes. Finally, Julianna and Wenona cited social structures, including social and educational policies, as potentially inciting and legitimizing violence. For example, Wenona discussed securitized responses to bullying as potentially promoting violence.

3   Exploring Enmity Together – Collaborative Learning

3.1   *Finding #6: Collaborative Learning Can Lead to New Understandings*
New understandings emerged from the collaborative and participatory approach, including diverse ways in which enmity can be constructed. For example, the majority of the participants questioned the photo of the "CAUTION!! Men Working in Lobby" sign. Many suggested the photo was about corporate expansion and competing interests. Rachel had a strong reaction

to the sign and questioned why a "gender specific sign" would be made and stated that the sign "screams inequality." Audrey shared "it's bad, it didn't even cross my mind. I actually didn't get that picture or why it was there until you pointed it out and I was like, oh yeah." After Isla described her intention with the photo (i.e., patriarchy as represented in *men* being written on the sign and symbolizing the exclusion of women) our group began to explore gendered elements of many of the photos as well as exploring how we are socialized differently based on race, gender, and age, for example. We discussed how our socialization in a patriarchal society, masks gendered constructions as *deficient,* regardless of gender. Isla also pointed out how these socializations are often deep within our subconscious suggesting "the person who made the sign probably didn't even think about it."

Another photo that led to much discussion was Lily's photo of a computer representing technology, specifically social media. Commenting on her peer's photo, Isla cautioned that "social media allows conflict to be faceless and more and more people can disconnect from their actions via the internet, via text ..." To illustrate her concern, Isla described watching a CBC documentary about unaccompanied minors in a course on migration. She described the anonymous, public comments that followed the on-line video: "people were saying things like the parents are probably terrorists sending them over first." Isla argued "these people would probably never say that or voice that in a room full of people, but because they can hide behind a screen name, they can voice those opinions." Audrey added "I read an article lately about how social media has allowed people to create the identity they want" and continued to elaborate on the fluidity of our identities. As a result of our group discussion, our focus on social media and enmity constructions broadened from citing incidents of inter-personal violence among peers via Facebook, to include the influence of our lived experiences and the role of anonymity in aiding and abetting violence (and peaceful processes) to emerge in new spaces.

Our collaborative learning was also evident when the youth participants would verbalize an increased understanding or a different perspective they had not considered before. For example, Rachel revealed the term *enemy* proved problematic for her but "when I came in and someone said 'Other', I never even thought of it from that perspective." Rachel described how her representations would have been different had we had the opportunity to explore *enemy* as a concept together before the photography activity. Similarly, Audrey shared that our collective learning enabled her to gain more depth and context into the representations of enmity. After hearing from Isla about the context of the 'spilled garbage can' photo, Audrey shared

> I like the picture of the garbage cans and I didn't really know until you pointed it out that people walked by and didn't pick it up. So like just being so apathetic that's an enemy and that's the source of so much conflict.

This exchange led to an additional conversation between Audrey and Isla who discussed how important multiple perspectives of shared experiences are because each person will see different things and there are opportunities within those differences.

After discussing the multiple perspectives envisioned in the participant generated photos, we engaged in a group discussion about key quotes (as determined by each participant). Audrey responded to a quote by Ziko who discussed the process of dehumanization as the inability to see the humanity in another (Ziko had acknowledged authorship of the quote). Audrey agreed with Ziko and added,

> even just look at the way the media portrays terrorists. They are not people, they are terrorists. And if you can dehumanize someone it is easier to kill them, or like in a battle the enemy is not a person, the enemy is the enemy – a monster.

While Audrey's photos and key messages focused on violence (and peace) in her everyday activities, engaging in a group dialogue allowed her to consider violence in relation to combatants in an armed conflict. The exchange between Ziko and Audrey revealed the interconnections between interpersonal and international levels of violence and highlighted the importance of engaging in dialogue with people who have diverse lived experience.

In addition to the participant quotes I also displayed key quotes from the professional informants (PI) in relation to enmity constructions for the youth to use when and as they wished (or not at all). I provided an opportunity for the participants to read the quotes from the PIs and occasionally highlighted a quote during our discussions when relevant connections arose. The youth participants routinely ventured to the table displaying these quotes and would read or refer to certain ideas during our large group discussions. For example, Amya argued that "media influences constructions of enmity" and referred to Chester's quote about journalism to highlight the connection: "very few journalists provide the analysis that goes behind the story it's just sound bites and clips and headlines" (Chester, PI). In response to Amya's argument, we engaged in a conversation about what society is asking of journalism and wondered if our drive for immediate satisfaction, our focus on violence versus conflict, and our willingness to emphasize difference over commonality, drives this kind of journalism. Ziko disagreed, stating "those stories [critical perspective with deep analysis] are definitely out there, it just depends on where you are accessing your media." Isla agreed, stating "I think it is more mainstream media. I think that's where you are frustrated ... because there are like Al Jeezera and Democracy Now. They are a little bit more free thinking ... whereas like CNN and Fox News ... are just talking heads." In this regard, Audrey made a link to her quote "the enemy is not a person but the evil behind it" and suggested

> perhaps the culture behind journalism and the media right now is that [referring to increased free-lance work, low pay, limited support] ... Like that's a problem if that is the way it is – the burden on journalists to produce these works with no pay ... it's not about the individual [journalist] it's about the system.

Our discussion about the role of media in influencing identity constructions moved from the work of individual journalists or particular news stations, to consider the contexts and various powers involved in news development and dissemination. In this regard, Rachel discussed the changing nature of news, cautioning the validity of news stemming from social media while at the same time highlighting the advantages of getting the "news directly from the actual people." Finally, Audrey questioned if we "are educating people and giving them skills to do that [find alternative, critical media sources] in the first place?"

4 Conclusions and Discussions

In this chapter, I have demonstrated the complexity of identity constructions of *enemy* as understood by the youth participants. The following five findings are foundational in the construction of enmity: (1) Identity(ies) as Different – Deficient; (2) Disengaged Citizenship; (3) Systems of Exclusion; (4) Normalizations of Violence; and (5) Competition and Rivalry. I also shared key messages about constructions of the *dehumanized other* – the *enemy* – from the perspective of the professional informants and highlighted the connections between the youth's perspectives and the perspectives shared by the PIs. Moreover, I discussed the 6th finding: (6) Collaborative learning can lead to new understandings about enmity constructions. Sharing diverse perspectives within safe(r) learning spaces are important methodological and pedagogical considerations for deepening an analysis of enmity. Our collaborative approach embraced Thayer-Bacon's (2003) emphasis on relational epistemologies and the importance of relationality and learning together. In the next chapter, I share our collaborative analysis process of exploring how power influences constructions of enmity.

Notes

1. Due to the participants' disappointment with the quality of the disposable camera photos, hand-drawn participant approved images are used to maintain the essence of the visual, arts-based methodologies utilized in our research process.
2. A 'selfie' is a photo of oneself, often taken by oneself.
3. Raymond Taavel was murdered in 2012 by an individual who was on a temporary release from The Nova Scotia Hospital. The Nova Scotia Hospital provides a broad range of mental health programs. Following Mr. Taavel's death, members of the community of Halifax created a community garden to honour his life and his advocacy for the LGBTQ community (CBC, 2015d).
4. Cornwallis was a British officer who became the first Governor of Nova Scotia. He was heralded as a founder of Halifax and honoured with statutes, schools titles and street names. His legacy has been challenged within the past 20 years due to the violence he perpetrated on Mi'kmaq peoples. As a result of advocacy work challenging historical representations of Cornwallis, some school and building site names have been changed (Canadian Encyclopedia, 2015).
5. The Voice is a televised singing competition.
6. The quotes were not attributed to specific individuals.
7. Pseudonyms are used for PIs to protect identity.

CHAPTER 8

Exploring Power Assumptions *with* Youth

> [Power] is like a giant pinball machine moving around and moving from place to place and through scales and actors. And so we have to be attentive and think very carefully about how we are reading power.
> MEI (RESEARCH PI)

∴

Power is part of all social relationships (Foucault, 2000; Mullaly, 2010) and thus, is deeply rooted within learning processes and knowledge mobilization (Freire, 1970). In order to explore how power influences the constructions of enmity, and consequently, how power influences strategies for changing these constructions, it was important for our group to name how we feel, see, and understand power operating in our everyday lives. Explicitly teaching about power, knowledge constructions, and socialization are important foundations toward building *critical consciousness* and for creating opportunities for social change (Freire, 1970; Kirby, Greaves, & Reid, 2010; Susskind, 2010). "Understanding power in relation to the external environment … how power operates in different ways to shape a problem" is an essential area of focus within critical adult education and a key area of focus of this study (Hunjan & Pettit, 2011, p. 26). Thus, exploring normalizations of violence within a power analysis brings hidden and invisible mechanisms which support violence to the surface, so critique and transformation is possible. This chapter highlights the participants power assumptions.

1   Power and Agency

Several participants described power as operating through actors and being of and in the individual. Opal shared "despite your position in structural ways and all that, individuals do have agency and can change their position and affect things." Rachel suggested "power is through individual action" and added "individual decisions add to a social power that creates structures." Furthermore, Crystal claimed "no one can change your situation, except for you" and suggested power is like an "upside-down pyramid and it all comes down to the people ... the individual is how power is perceived on a larger scale."

Lily also perceived power as operating through people and represented power as something owned or possessed. For instance, Lily asked "who has power and who is given power?" and she further suggested, "if you're fighting you have power over someone else, if you're winning, I guess." In relation to dominance and power over, Lily asked the group to consider: "how do we be in those experiences of power and try to even the battlefield ... without exerting more domination and exacerbating the problem? How do we get out of these situations where people are constantly trying to dominate other people?" Amya also referred to dominance, sharing, "we can let people have power over us." And Kira stated "somebody has to be in power. Somebody has to have it but I think it's entirely how it's used."

With regard to assumptions and opportunities for change, Rachel argued "change would start with individual action and relationships but where you would actually see change is between these two areas [social structure and cultural change]." Similarly, Lily reflected on our work in Even Wars Have Limits (EWHL), teaching and learning about armed conflict and international humanitarian issues, stating: "we don't frame it as power over ... we talk about vulnerable people but we don't talk about power structures." Both Lily and Rachel held strong agency perspectives, however, as we began to share diverse understandings, they began to discuss more interconnections between agency, relations, structures and cultural norms.

2   Power and Relations

The participants who saw power operating in a relational capacity challenged the agential perspective of their peers. For example, Audrey stated "I take the point that it all comes down to people, but I believe it is about the relations between the people where power is actually seen. And how you negotiate power between people that creates structures, that creates social boundaries." Additionally, Isla discussed how power would not exist with one individual, but power comes into play when issues of dominance and power over are created, a process she sees as occurring within relations. To illustrate this point, Audrey claimed

> I think it all starts here [relations]. Policy doesn't exist except in relations; people do not make change without connecting to others. Like Martin

FIGURE 8.1 "Using your power in a positive way to build each other up." – Audrey

Luther King was not powerful himself, he was powerful because he was able to connect and that's how culture shifts.

For Audrey, power also exists within relations among people and God. She claimed "how I understand power – it actually comes from my faith ... and it really all comes back to love." She described the positive potential in relations of power and shared a picture of her parents holding hands to illustrate her argument (Figure 8.1). She discussed how relations of power can be viewed from a community lens, where people can use "your power in a positive way to build each other up." She also elaborated on her power and love representation, sharing, "power in the sense of what it can add to your life and what it can add to the people around you."

Participants raised questions about *power over, power with, power within* and *power to*,[1] emulating the Expressions of Power as discussed by Veneklasen and Miller (2002). In the illustration above, Audrey saw power as predominantly in the expression of *power with*. Another participant shared an anonymous comment during the focus group written evaluations, arguing power exists in relations. The participant wrote:

> most enemies arise from power struggles. These power struggles are prevalent at all levels (personal, organizational, structural). Seems people really believe it is up to the individual to make a difference, but I think this is very problematic for places that value community as most important.

For this participant, power is a complex concept, which stems beyond the individual and is located in multiple spaces, particularly within relations.

3 Power and Social Structure

While Audrey spoke largely of power as operating within relations, she also raised a caution in favour of a structural view:

> I don't know if I would completely agree that it is with the individual because you need the structures to access the individual. Education is the best example. Yeah individuals can create change but they need the skills, they need the awareness to create change. So if we say it's all on you to make change and not provide that support. How can we expect that?

Amya focused on how power is operating within social structures raising concerns about systemic racism and discrimination. Amya argued that while "structure is created by the people," it is beyond individual agency. As for assumptions about change and power, she claimed, "I think policy is what is going to make sustainable change and that stems from all of these" [i.e. relations, agency, and culture].

4 *Explicitly* Exploring Assumptions of Power Is Key for Collaborative Social Action

The discussion above captured the early conversations between participants who were sharing their views about power for the first time (see Table 8.1). The purpose of exploring our assumptions about how power operates was not

TABLE 8.1 How power operates – youth perspectives

Youth participants	How power operates
Audrey	Power can be positive.
Ziko	Power is about influence.
Crystal	Dominating power is accepted as normal.
Dexie	Power shapes how we communicate.
Lily, Isla & Rachel	Power is personal agency.
Opal	Power can be in the form of resistance.
Kira	Power is owned and used.
Amya	Power is about social position and social structure.

to come to a consensus on power, but to understand how our assumptions guide our analysis and plans for social action. The conversations among the youth were rich and critical. One participant wrote on an anonymous evaluation: "I learned a lot about the way we conceptualize power individually and as a society." Another participant wrote: "I think it is very important to remember that opinions and feelings about power and enmity are subjective and very complex."

The participants revealed diverse and contradictory understandings of power. Observing these contradictions brought our group discussion back to our community standards and our commitment to recognizing that all *knowledge is partial*. We spent a significant amount of time discussing our assumptions about power and how change occurs, a conversation that the youth suggested they had not had intentionally before. It was important for us to see how we each understand power, as our assumptions and understandings of power yielded differing ideas around socialization processes. The representations of power and the strategies for change, as identified by the youth, were often contradictory and lead to important conversations about the theories supporting our critical educational work.

5 Frameworks for Analyzing Power

To begin our exploration of how power influences enmity constructions, I shared multiple frameworks and organizations of how power operates. We explored the *Forms of Power: visible, hidden, invisible,* using the *Power Cube;* for instance, whether we can see power (e.g. creation of laws), or know power exists despite not being explicitly revealed (e.g. the ability to manipulate agendas), or power that lies deep within beliefs and values, shaping our norms (e.g. discriminatory jokes and stereotypes that perpetuate social exclusion) (Gaventa, 2006). We explored *Expressions of Power: power to, power with* and *power within,* as a framework where power is animated as the ability to create change, the ability to work with others for change, or the value and confidence within oneself to create change (Veneklasen & Miller, 2002). We explored Hayward's (2000) *de-facing power* where power is not about questions of distribution or individual choice; but rather, "how do power's mechanisms define the (im)possible, the natural, the normal, what counts as a 'problem'?" (p. 35). The participants also discussed the Onion analysis as a means to delve deeper into the multiple influences involved in constructing and maintaining (or challenging) negative constructions of other and decided to utilize this framework due to their familiarity with it.

6   'The Onion' Analysis

The Onion is an analytical tool designed to raise awareness and understanding about the factors that fuel and/or challenge a particular social problem from a personal, organizational, or societal level (Figure 8.2) (Hunjan & Pettit, 2011).

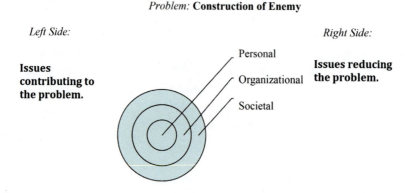

FIGURE 8.2   The onion analysis (adapted from Hunjan & Pettit, 2011)

We used *The Onion* to build on, and bring together, all of our previous work (including the photos, journals, and interviews), to begin to consider the mechanisms of power and strategies for building peace. Using the participant generated photos, the youth key messages, the key messages from the professional informants, and the group discussions, the participants engaged in a deep level discussion about our problem – how power influences the construction of enmity – and the forms of power *fuelling* and *challenging* this social problem.

When tasked with exploring what *fuels* and *challenges* constructions of enmity, the participants drew upon their photos for inspiration and described their heightened sense for *seeing* power, particularly as a result of the photography exercise and the corresponding discussions. One participant shared in an anonymous evaluation:

> I think that throughout the entire project, from taking pictures to our discussion today, I really learned to reflect more on what power can look like and how it is enacted in so many different ways. And that reflection is so important in building the foundation to move forward.

In fact, the participants joked about wearing *power glasses*,[2] which enabled them to "see things" (operations of power in dehumanized constructions of other) that they had not seen before. They discussed the permanency of their new and enhanced *power glasses* and their inability to remove them even when they just wished to be "ignorant" (Rachel). The participants described the *power glasses* as an important critical tool, but an equally burdensome tool, as critical perspectives are not always welcome by family and peers.

The process of analyzing the construction of an enemy proved challenging as the focus was abstract in comparison to a particular community-based social problem. Amya raised an important point about context, stating: "when you are talking about peace and conflict your approach has to be different depending on where you are ... you can't even have the same conversation or use the same language." During this process, the participants appeared to transition back and forth between *forms* of power and *expressions of power*, highlighting the complexities involved in evaluative frameworks exploring power. They seemed to associate *forms* of power with the construction of enmity, and the *expressions of power* with the development of peacebuilding strategies. Given that the participants shared social action as an expectation of the research process, it is not surprising that a significant portion of their analysis focused on strategies as illustrated using *expressions of power*.

Power Over

The youth participants described power over, or domination, as being fundamental in the construction of enmity, naming greed, patriarchy, racism, homophobia, and aspirations for control over resources as root issues. The participants discussed how social and economic injustice create an, us-versus-them mentality, leading to inequity, or benefits for a few, and negative impacts for most. The youth referred to their photos depicting systems of exclusion (i.e. sign of men working) and competition and rivalry (i.e. competing corner stores) to illustrate power over.

In relation to unlearning enmity, the youth identified critical education as a key strategy to challenge *power over*, by naming and identifying the spaces and forms of "dominant" power in social learning processes. Examples of non-inclusive curriculum, and traditional (or non-democratic) teacher-student relationships were used to animate *power over* within learning processes fuelling enmity (Table 8.2). In this regard, Kira argued it is important to

> understand the story of how they got there [the dominant person – the enemy]. You need to try and explain how somebody got to where they are. Maybe there is a story of how someone got to be doing what they are doing ... It is easy to dismiss someone as an enemy.

TABLE 8.2 Youth participants – strategies for peace

Expression of power	Strategies for peace
Power over	– Critical education – naming & identifying spaces and forms of power in learning processes. – Critical thinking and explicitly learning power. – Exploring history & the story behind the "dominance."
Power with	– Forming relations between people, particularly people in conflict. – Focus on respectful and equitable relations. – Finding common goals and common spaces.
Power within	– More attention to focused on developing a state of peacefulness, or "being at peace," and increasing confidence to create change. – Challenge disempowerment by focusing on the *power to* people and communities have to create change. – Exploring confidence and self-efficacy with youth.
Power to	– Empowered individuals. – Critical thinking and critical literacy skills. – Global issues awareness. – Conflict transformation skills (ex. conflict assessment).

For Kira, exploring relations of power is key for creating opportunities for peace.

In addition, Rachel discussed power over, in the context of racism and stereotyping. She claimed "stereotypes can impact what you are allowed to do and what resources you can access." Rachel suggested that challenging enmity constructions directly can lead to a change in perspective and a change in power. For example, she claimed,

> you can tear it down [racist comment] by saying 'excuse me that offended me like on a massive level and it also offended this group of people. We feel really offended that you've done that.' And I think by doing that you can change the power structure back.

Rachel argued that racism is so deeply rooted in our culture that the first step to challenge this hidden and invisible form of "negative" power is to expose it.

Power With

In addition to *power over*, the participants described the lack of *power with* as a substantial contribution to dehumanizing the other. They discussed *power with* in relation to disassociations and disengaged citizenship, claiming if people with opposing views made connections, constructing the other as an enemy would be more difficult. Opal started the conversation in her group describing positive relations, for example, "getting to know someone" as a means to reduce enmity constructions. Audrey shared, "you would think that with all of the innovative stuff that we have it all comes back to getting people in the same room." Crystal suggested "just being in the same space working towards the same goal ... trying to find common goals and common space" can lead to power with. Finally, Opal argued "The only way for people to stop othering each other, and stop hating each other, is getting to know each other and getting to love each other in some kind of way."

At the same time, Isla claimed that "you have to have social capital to make change," lamenting that some groups have opportunity for "legitimate participation" while others are excluded. In her example, Isla focused on hidden forms of power within *power with* and inequitable relations of power that exist in communities, including learning communities. For example, nationalism was discussed as a system of inclusion and exclusion. On the one hand nationalism generates *power with* or feelings of connection to work together (in some cases). On the other hand, Isla (and other participants) described nationalism as an unnatural barrier to global/peaceful citizenship and cautioned about the underlying ideology supporting the creation and protection of borders.

Power Within

Power within was a focus of our conversation from the beginning photography activity. The youth discussed how personal experience, including fearful experiences, can impact confidence and constructions of the negative other. Audrey shared, the "biggest difficulty is rallying people out of feeling disempowered. People can get so overwhelmed with the content so it is focusing on the things we can do to make positive change. That is the work." The youth also described "being at peace" as a *power within* to make a difference. There was a common agreement among the youth that *power within* was an under discussed, and underrepresented form of power within education discourse on conflict, and an area requiring further discussion in relation to the work of the EWHL team.

Power To

In relation to the work of the Even Wars Have Limits volunteers, the concept of *power to* was an important consideration. Majority of EWHL work revolved around empowering individuals to create positive social change. For example, Isla shared:

> What I get out of it, and I don't know what you guys get out of it, but it comes down to the empowerment of the individual to make the choice. To choose whether or not to be a contributing factor [to violence] or a reducing factor and how they process those choices is dependent upon which organizations they are part of and which kind of social structures they connect with.

Similarly, Audrey suggested that our priority should be to "empower young people to make that decision to be able to read about international law, about land mines so they have a frame of reference to make educated choices or have educated opinions [on issues of violence]."

The youth participants saw *power to* as being an essential focus to challenge constructions of other and named particular knowledge and skills required to help develop global active and peaceful citizens, including: awareness of international issues, critical literacy skills, and conflict transformation skills such as non-violent communication. The youth also discussed an EWHL workshop, entitled *Active Global Citizenship* (AGC), that they frequently facilitated with younger youth as part of their volunteer work. The goal of this workshop centered on empowerment, and identifying the skills, experiences, resources, and relations that individuals (in this case youth) have to create change. The participants spoke positively about the need for workshops like AGC to be incorporated in peacebuilding education, particularly with youth. For the participants, the AGC workshop encompassed aspects of *power within, power with* and *power to*, with the possibility of reformatting to enhance the *power with* focus to privilege respectful and equitable relations. The youth participants held diverse and contradictory assumptions about power and social change, but they all held a strong assumption about the possibilities for an educational approach to building peace.

7 Expressions and Forms of Power

Throughout the power analyses process, the participants reflected on the complexity of power and the difficulty associated with applying power concepts to real life problems. While the language of *Expressions of Power* was favoured by the participants, they also described *hidden* power and in some cases began to uncover *invisible* forms of power in their examples. For instance,

Opal argued, "money itself is not the power issue, it is what people will do for it." In an alternative example, Isla discussed the importance of innovation and "changing in a positive way" and encouraged her peers to think beyond what we see now, but to consider new possibilities moving forward, particularly given our discussion around hegemony and internalized norms. In this regard, Rachel favored the formal school system as "the best structure we have already to create change." However, Opal disagreed stating, "education [school] is in the realm of what already is, so how can you make changes if that's what's messed up?" Lily added to this comment, claiming enmity constructions can be challenged "by a shift in attitude or way of thinking" or a whole new system. These comments connect to Hicks' (2004) assertion that "much teaching about contemporary issues, quite rightly, tends to focus on the problem in hand, but often neglects exploration of the preferred alternative states that need to be worked towards" (p. 171). One could argue the "preferred alternative states" are communities free of hegemony where equitable living is valued and experienced.

Notes

1 Power over, power with, and power to is an interpretation on power, from an agential perspective, as described within the Power Spectrum (Veneklasen & Miller, 2002).
2 I believe it was Lily who coined the term *power glasses*, but it was a term that several participants referred to during our focus groups.

CHAPTER 9

Strategies for Building Cultures of Peace *with* Youth

> Young people should be at the forefront of global change and innovation. Empowered, they can be key agents for development and peace. If, however, they are left on society's margins, all of us will be impoverished. Let us ensure that all young people have every opportunity to participate fully in the lives of their societies.
>
> KOFI ANNAN

∴

To tie all of our learning together, we created a theory of change according to how the youth participants believe violence transformation and peacebuilding can occur. This theory of change was based on the work of Anderson (n.d.) who uses *backward mapping,* beginning with the goal and working outward toward the strategies. We explored the *ingredients* or *building blocks* required to build cultures of peace within our communities. We also identified the indicators, which would reveal our successes and failures in this effort (Figure 9.1). During this process the youth reflected on their past public engagement[1] work and reflected on how they regularly developed strategies without considering the building blocks or the indicators of peace explicitly, a practice they hoped to include in future planning.

FIGURE 9.1   Theory of change – youth strategies for building cultures of peace

1 The Goal: Building Cultures of Peace

The majority of our time together involved an explicit focus on violence, including the constructions of the dehumanized other (enemy) and the mechanism maintaining normalizations of violence. When it came time to plan for action and change, the youth switched gears to focus instead on where we want to go and what change we want to see – a focus on peacebuilding.

Prior to beginning, Rachel raised important cautions about language and our need to define key concepts as a foundation of our theory of change. Rachel argued "it is really difficult to define what peace is. It is almost easier to define what the conflict is and then peace is just the removal of that conflict a lot of times." Amya disagreed, stating "conflict can be an opportunity. I have a problem when people see peace without conflict. I think we can have peace with conflict, but it is having the tools to deal with conflict." Audrey added:

> there is literature around the idea of a culture of peace that challenges the idea that peace is the absence of something. [Rachel agreed, saying – "right"] but rather it is the positive presence of something else… it is even how we talk about conflict. Our goal is not to get rid of the conflict, it is to replace it.

We used backwards mapping in the development of our theory of change and identified cultures of peace as our end goal, again, using the UN definition[2] as our guide. For the youth, cultures of peace included the following: equity, empathy, justice and freedom, respectful relations, community centered engagement, intergenerational learning and living, free from violence, and conflict resolution (Figure 9.2).

CULTURES OF PEACE
Conflict Resolution
Free from Violence
Intergenerational Living
Community Centered
Respectful Relationships
Freedom & Justice
Empathy
Equity

FIGURE 9.2   Theory of change: goal – building cultures of peace

Within our focus on building cultures of peace, Audrey asked us to consider the role of intergenerational cooperation because "youth can create a lot of change, but in the absence of other generations is change possible? It is a systems thing, we keep generations separated." Rachel added that in order to create change people must be open to change, stating "fear of change is one of the biggest promoters [of violence]."

2 What is Needed for Cultures of Peace?

Our next step involved identifying what we need in place to achieve cultures of peace. We used sticky notes to capture *precursors* to peace and to allow for editing. The responses ranged from individual perspectives such as Amya's assertion that "my culture of peace would be one where I can be myself," to Rachel's suggestion that education is a necessary precursor for building cultures of peace, as education can provide "a platform for coming together." Audrey argued for a "governing structure" which lead to heated discussions about what kind of governance structures most closely aligns with the vision of cultures of peace as created by the youth. The final conclusion was a democratic government, however another conversation ensued about the definition of democracy.

Amya discussed the importance of collaborative living and dialogue in relation to building cultures of peace. She stated:

> I wrote dialogue and collaboration and we didn't really talk about it but where those two words for me stemmed from was like living in a society with multiple cultures and how do we have a culture of peace with multiple cultures when there is different standards and different values. So having an open dialogue about that and having a collaborative approach so that everybody is like you know this is going to vary depending on the different cultures within that.

The participants described several precursors, or *things* that are needed to build cultures of peace. The precursors included: socially responsible markets; participatory education; democratic governance; engaged citizens; restorative law enforcement; diverse and collective communities; freedom to be yourself; safe communities; basic needs being met; health care; and a legal/policy framework. This was presented as the youths' ideal towards achieving cultures of peace. The full list of precursors are captured below.

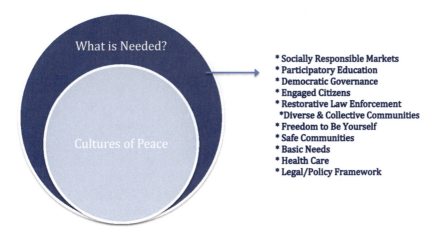

FIGURE 9.3   What is needed for cultures of peace?

3   Measuring Progress towards Cultures of Peace

While we spent time building our holistic idea of what cultures of peace might look like, as educators we were focused on building an educational framework within a broader theory of change, and thus, we discussed the next steps generally in relation to all precursors before zooming in on education specifically. The youth felt it was important to capture a holistic picture of our culture of peace to frame the kind of educational theory of change we were aspiring to create. The indicators for each precursor were discussed generally. For example, when I asked what *restorative law enforcement* would look like in a culture of peace, Rachel responded by saying, "what we all thought that Canada's military was like when we were children [peacekeepers]." In measurable terms, the youth determined we could measure our progress in the area of *restorative law enforcement,* by the following criteria: reduced use of weapons; enhanced positive public opinion of law enforcement, including approachability and trustworthiness; use of non-violent interventions; equitable and respectful relations.

4   Respectful and Equitable Relations Are Building Blocks for Cultures of Peace

The youth suggested "respectful and equitable relations is an indicator for all else [all building blocks for cultures of peace]." When I asked "what relationships mean in relation to a culture of peace … what kind of relationships are

- **Socially Responsible Markets** - people have more rights than markets; corporate social responsibility; accountability to citizens; equitable & respectful relations
- **Participatory Education** - lifelong learning; informed people; equitable & respectful relations
- **Democratic Governance** - access to vote; all voices heard; accountable & responsible to citizens; equitable & respectful relations with citizens
- **Engaged Citizens** - informed people; equitable & respectful relations; youth engagement; voting (participation is a starting point); active & civic involvement; mind, heart, body; intergenerational
- **Restorative Law Enforcement** - reduced use of weapons; positive public opinion; accessible; use of non-violent interventions; equitable & respectful relations
- **Diverse & Collective Communities** - equitable & respectful relations; multicultural; open-mindedness; shared spaces/community
- **Freedom to Be Yourself** - diverse identities; see & value variety of identities & beliefs; equitable & respectful relations
- **Safe Communities** - free from violence; equitable & respectful relations
- **Basic Needs** - people are fed, have clean drinking water & are sheltered
- **Health Care** - healthy people - mind, body & soul
- **Legal/Policy Framework (HR)** - represents diversity; policy & legislation that support our culture of peace (Human Rights Framework)

FIGURE 9.4 Measuring progress towards cultures of peace

we talking about?" the youth collectively shared: respectful, equitable, and non-violent relationships. Rachel responded "it's like the whole paper [theory of change] should be called relationships and everything else should be put on top of that." The discussion on indicators varied from precursor to precursor, however a focus on relationships, remained central.

In relation to education, the participants saw education as connected to all the precursors yet they created a particular section focusing on *participatory education*. They suggested *participatory education* would be realized if the following outcomes were achieved: (1) appreciation for and active engagement in lifelong learning; (2) informed people, informed on local and global issues; and (3) the privileging of equitable and respectful relations. The measurements for each precursor are listed in Figure 9.4.

5   Strategies for Cultures of Peace

The youth created a complex picture of their ideal culture of peace, recognizing the *fuellers* and *challengers* to violence, including how forms of power operate within violence (and peace). Reflecting on power and the development of our theory of change, Audrey shared:

> I wonder if that is the piece that brings this into reality, it's where the power sits. Like we can design something like this [*Theory of Change*] and assume equitable power throughout but what if one of these things has more power than the other and how does that shape our culture of peace?

Rachel added, "We are figuring out power every step of this." For Audrey and Rachel, they felt that the holistic vision of a culture of peace was important but recognized "in the real world" different precursors would carry different weight depending on "where the power sits." This was an important conversation, highlighting the areas in society where power is most "held" such as the military and law enforcement structures.

For the next step, identifying the strategies to achieve cultures of peace, we re-engaged with the *Power Cube* to consider spaces for intervention and possible transformations (Gaventa, 2006). Amya raised an important caution: "it is one thing to talk about conflict resolution and peace education in a classroom setting and another to be able to like take a real life moment and take that opportunity to educate." She described a conflict between two colleagues that stemmed from ideological differences and how her team, who were all trained conflict resolution educators, struggled to support a peaceful conversation in the midst of the conflict. Amya's example enabled the group to discuss the contexts for their peacebuilding educational strategies and the importance of working with youth and adults, in both formal and non-formal sites.

The participants discussed how their work with EWHL provided an important balance of working within formal education (invited spaces) and community (created spaces) and yet, they identified many sites that were unavailable to them (closed spaces). The closed spaces identified ranged from the lack of youth engaged in curriculum development within the formal education system to the lack of youth leadership within organizations such as the Canadian Red Cross. Furthermore, Audrey discussed the importance of dialogue and safe spaces and wondered if "the classroom is where they [youth] talk or is it a place they feel obligated to go?" Our discussion about invited, closed, and created spaces included the recognition of how power operates within these spaces. Within both focus groups, an interesting debate ensued between those who privileged strategies focusing on empowering individuals (*power to*) and those who privileged relations (*power with*) as the most effective route to create cultures of peace. The debate is captured in the following sections.

6 Empowered Individuals – Engaged Citizens

In relation to education, and creating pedagogies for peace, Audrey asked "what is the best way to inform young people, what the best way is to inform them on the issues? … How do young people access information?" She also stated: "hearing what everyone is saying we always come back to the individual, empowering individual people … but what do we mean by engaged? … personal reflections? … some sort of change involved?" Within the focus on empowered individuals, the group debated whether awareness or engagement was most important. Audrey captured the debate, saying: "it's the chicken and the egg. Do you get people active first or do you teach them and then get them active?"

Rachel indicated that the focus should be "the way EWHL goes about it … through awareness raising and educational practice." Rachel further stated, "When you inform youth, you can inform the family too." Amya agreed, suggesting,

> Maybe they are not going to be a fully engaged citizen but it is good to have some awareness … informing people is where we are going to see that activity and that activism extend from. It's almost like you have to inform them before… that information is the building block for their activism.

Audrey disagreed, sharing:

> When I talk about engaged citizens, it doesn't mean people who just show up it means people who care. So when I think about EWHL and the stuff we talk about and the awareness we want to raise, we are not just doing it for information sake, at least for me personally. I go into it thinking, how can I engage young people in the topic and thus becoming engaged citizens so they are no longer participants in their society, but they are actively engaged themselves. Education is a piece

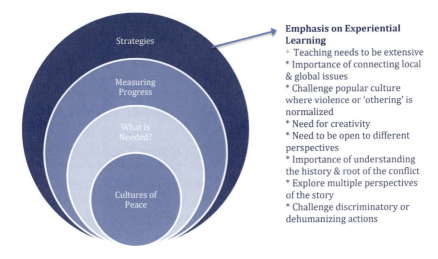

FIGURE 9.5   Strategies for building cultures of peace

of that, but not the end goal. At least for me. My end goal is to see young people get involved and to engage.

The participants provided examples of engagement including: challenging discriminatory actions, exploring multiple perspectives on issues of peace and violence, using creative non-violent practices, and challenging violence embedded within popular culture (Figure 9.5).

For the youth participants, empowering individuals also includes the ability to connect local and global issues of violence within a critical lens. Lily argued,

> in the way we teach it [*international humanitarian law*] we tend to overlook ... um even like things like having guns in the house or violent video games we tend to overlook when teaching about child soldiers how to relate that to children playing with guns here [*Canada*]. We fail to connect it when we are teaching about it ... why are we so desensitized to kids running around hitting each other with sticks or playing with guns? When we know like, children in war is wrong, we know that but there is no connection between it. So I think that is one of the biggest teaching failures is the connection.

Other participants emphasized the importance of making connections as well. Amya shared, "we can have peace with conflict but we need to have the tools to deal with conflict." And Rachel added, "there are a lot of things people are using to create peace and they don't even realize it."

7 Peaceful Relations

The participants also saw the ability to engage in respectful relations as a primary strategy towards building cultures of peace. The youth who privileged relations, spoke of the importance of peacebuilding education being extensive throughout formal and non-formal education, including among youth, among adults, and between youth and adults. Rachel suggested that we need to return to the lessons of our early childhood to explore respectful relations. For example, she claimed, "we have gotten away from some of the most basic things like sharing … sharing is caring." Rachel also raised an important point, claiming: "you are capable of achieving peace, you are not destined or you are not obligated to be peaceful … understanding that, how do we allow a way for people to achieve peaceful relationships?"

Audrey focused on the importance of authenticity in relationships. She argued that we need to "walk the walk" and shared examples of people "who sing these beautiful songs of worship but yet exploit the poor." Being in respectful relations involves the ability and willingness to be open to different perspectives.

8 Experiential Learning

In the end, the youth agreed that the combination of awareness (for example, how power operates in constructions of the dehumanized other), engagement (for example, challenging enmity constructions), and respectful relations (for example, practicing peace skills such as non-violent communication) were essential to building cultures of peace. In considering how to develop educational strategies that incorporate these three aspects, the youth kept coming back to a particular quote shared by Ning, one of the professional informants: "bridge the empathy gap … lack of empathy of other living experiences and conditions that prevents us from having empathy and getting engaged to try and improve."

Amya argued that experiential learning is an effective strategy to "bridge the empathy gap." She stated experiential education enables opportunities to "build empathy and understanding and try and put them in a simulated situation and that starts the engagement. They are now relating to it. In their own personal way they have made a connection to it." Audrey agreed, sharing "why we would want to do experiential learning is to allow young people the ability to relate to the issues, open up perspectives, and build empathy and understanding." Rachel added "it is so important. It opens perspectives... it gives you the ability to actually take in more information." Rachel also shared:

> The use of experiential learning alone is not enough. The use of debriefing helps. It's the combination of those things. If you just use it on its own it can lead to exploiting and keeping people from being engaged but once you attach that to real experience through debrief and people can express that, you can explain things more clearly... but people can't understand the full thing ... If you use it on its own then it can lead to exploitation as well as keeping people disengaged from reality.

Amya cautioned, it "depends on the audience and the subject matter... and we have to think carefully about exploitation."

Opal suggested that the work of EWHL embraced all of these strategies (awareness raising, engagement, and relationship building) and that a re-vamp of the Active Global Citizenship (AGC) workshop, including the spaces where we offered this learning opportunity, ought to be considered as a strategy toward building cultures of peace. Opal argued that long-term relationships between young adult humanitarian educators and the youth who would participate in the workshop would enhance the sustainability of this pedagogical approach. Amya suggested a merging of Paxium[3] and AGC to bring together awareness raising, practicing peaceful and relational skills, and opportunities to practice engagement. In closing, the youth summarized their theory of change for building cultures of peace as:

> Our assumptions about working toward a culture of peace is that engaged citizens will help us reach that. We define engaged citizens by these things: informed people (informed on local and global social issues); respectful and equitable relations (including non-violent conflict transformation), participatory citizens; civic involvement (voice), active citizens, and inter-generational citizenships.

The youth emphasized experiential learning as a specific strategy, privileging empathy and understanding of diverse experiences. It is important to re-state the opportunity for action and reflection on peacebuilding pedagogies and spaces for developing peaceful processes was compromised due to an abrupt program cut at the Canadian Red Cross.

9 Discussion & Conclusions: Where Do We Go from Here?

As presented by the youth participants, the *enemy* or *dehumanized other*, is constructed within complex cultural and social contexts. Normalizations of violence, complex and contradictory identities, systems of exclusion, competition and rivalry, and disengaged citizenship were all presented as key contributors to enmity constructions. While the participants lacked racial and gender diversity, their unique lived experiences were evident in their understandings of enmity, and the shared learnings greatly contributed to the depth of the explorations about enmity constructions among young adults.

Stemming from their power analyses of violence and constructions of the *dehumanized other*, the youth developed a theory of change framed within an educational approach. The youth argue teaching and learning for peace ought to be rooted in critical and relational epistemologies as an essential strategy towards building cultures of peace. They identified adult education sites where opportunities exist for creating social change towards non-violence, conflict transformation, and respect for human dignity.

Notes

1. It is important to emphasize, this theory of change was developed more generally as a result of the abrupt closure of the youth-led humanitarian education programming at the Canadian Red Cross.
2. The UN (2002) define cultures of peace as "more than an absence of war ... it means justice and equity for all as the basis for living together in harmony and free from violence" (UNESCO, 2002, p. 1).
3. Paxium is an experiential workshop designed to engage participants as various characters in a conflict.

CHAPTER 10

Violence Transformation & Building Cultures of Peace

> Understanding the power of knowledge involves examining the power struggles among different knowledges.
>
> CAIRNS & SEARS, *The Democratic Imagination: Envisioning Popular Power inthe Twenty-First Century* (2012, p. 134)

∴

Violence is deeply embedded within society and is becoming increasingly complex (WHO, 2014), a phenomenon vividly captured by the youth participants in their analysis of enmity constructions. Exacerbated by globalization (Walby, 2009), and amplified within popular culture, the youth participants revealed the pervasiveness of violence, particularly within youth cultures. Yet spaces to critique violence and strategies for violence prevention are insufficient (WHO, 2014), and largely exclude the voices of youth. Understanding how violence (including dehumanization) is learned and becomes embedded in society, is essential to transform the *culture of violence*.

In this chapter, I present a relational approach to violence transformation and peacebuilding, which focuses on enhancing understandings of the normalizations of violence (power analyses), increasing critical pedagogical engagement (actively challenging how violence is learned), and developing participatory, peaceful processes. Within this approach, I discuss the value of naming power assumptions and processes for analyzing forms of power through critical reflection, dialogue, and relational pedagogies. I also discuss the importance of engaging young adults in peace work, within adult education, and reflect on the delicacy of analyzing the voices and perspectives of the youth participants in participatory research. Finally, I synthesize the principles of critical adult education (Freire, 1970), Galtung's (1996) peace epistemologies, and Thayer-Bacon's (2003) relational epistemology to discuss a pedagogical model for violence transformation.

1 Relational Approaches to Violence Transformation & Peacebuilding

How people come to *know reality* has been studied by many, and argued from many diverse philosophical positions. From Plato who privileged the mind, to Dewey who valued social experiences, the process of developing knowledge or truth(s) has been the focus of much debate and examination. Within this evolving debate, Berger and Luckmann (1996), argued for a sociological analysis of knowledge constructions, where learning is constructed in everyday social contexts. For Berger and Luckmann (1966), the sociology of knowledge "is concerned with the relationship between human thought and the social context within which it arises" (Berger & Luckmann, 1966, p. 3).

Stemming from this sociological analysis of learning, Thayer-Bacon (2003) argues that knowledge construction emerges within relations; that our sense of self and our "abilities to become knowers" develops through and in relationships (p. 7). Within this framework, knowledge is understood as socially constructed and negotiated, fluid, plural, and continuously changing (Bergum, 2003; Lange, 2015; Thayer-Bacon, 2003). This approach compliments, and likely stems from, indigenous and decolonizing epistemologies, where I/We/world relations are centered. Within indigenous and decolonizing epistemologies, knowledge is understood as being collective, shared, relational and deeply intertwined with relations of power (Chilisa, 2012; Mohanty, 2003; Smith, 1999).

A relational epistemology recognizes there is a relationship between knowing, and knowing together. Freire (1970) proposed the "world and human beings do not exist apart from each other, they exist in constant interaction" (p. 50). Similarly, Lange (2015) argues a relational lens is beyond a simplistic or dualistic view of self and society, but rather it involves individuals learning and developing as "individuals-in-relations, with the human and more-than-human world." In this sense, a relational epistemology derives from a relational ontology where connections between people and the natural world are paramount, again, sharing synergies with indigenous and decolonizing epistemologies and ontologies.

Within a relational lens, individuals are understood as having unique life experiences, always embedded within complex relations. Thus, individuals constitute an emergent self, including a core identity that evolves and changes in relation to others (Lange, 2015). In this regard, Cairns and Sears (2012) suggest,

> Each of us can only know the world from our own position within it. It is crucial, then, to listen to others who can inform us about how the world

looks from their vantage point. Through this dialogue and effective inquiry, we can figure out the ways in which individual experiences are shaped by forces beyond our own personal lives, so we can more clearly understand the uneven workings of the complex whole of society. (p. 133)

Studying how we learn within a relational epistemology, requires an analysis of embodied individuals, as learning is not "solely authored" (Thayer-Bacon, 2003, 2010). Beyond interactions with *others* and navigating "the world of irreducible differences," a relational epistemology also requires an internal exploration of the complexity of the self (Sidorkin, 2002, p. 153). Therefore, Bergum (2003) suggests, "the relational space (not the space where one or the other lives but the space that occurs between them) is where personal meaning is awakened and where inherent knowledge is developed" (p. 125).

Brownlee and Berthelsen (2008) argue a relational epistemology incorporates referential ("meaning") and structural ("organizational") dimensions (p. 409). The referential dimension focuses on the "relationship between knowers and the known" (Brownlee & Berthelsen, 2008, p. 410). For instance, the referential dimension considers how knowledge is conceived and evaluated (i.e. personal opinion, intuition, knowledge that is received by others and considered as truth, or theoretically derived knowledge) (Brownlee & Berthelsen, 2008). The structural dimension focuses on the organization of learning (i.e. centering on one element of a phenomenon with limited consideration for interconnecting elements, exploring multiple elements, or the interactions of multiple elements) (Brownlee & Berthelsen, 2008). According to Brownlee and Berthelsen (2008), teaching "needs to promote stronger connections between "the knower" and their existing beliefs and "the known" through internalisation of new knowledge that is evaluated and understood in a critical way" (p. 415). Therefore, the learning goal within a relational epistemology is not "how to overcome differences but, rather, with how to sustain its polyphony without losing any of the voices" (Sidorkin, 2002, p. 159). A relational epistemology includes a sociological analysis of the construction of knowledge, as well as a critical, yet plural analysis of the interconnections embedded within a particular phenomenon, in this case, the study of violence.

2 Relational, Peacebuilding Pedagogies

Peace work is rooted in relations. Thayer-Bacon (1999) argues "we can begin to build peace through acts of genuine caring" yet in order to genuinely care, we need to feel connected (p. 157). Sidorkin (2002) further argues that a relational pedagogy develops from the assumption that people have an inherent desire to belong. For Sidorkin (2002), relations are the center of education, and as educators we should be evaluating our *success* not in terms of what we do, but rather in the kind of relations we construct with the ultimate focus being on "our communal life" (p. 135). While Sidorkin's work focuses on children and youth in relation to formal schooling, his work on relational pedagogies is equally applicable to the study and practice of adult education. In fact, Brookfield (2005) contends "the task of adult education is to break the chains of illusion that bind people to an individualized view of life" (p. 174).

Feeling connected to *others* was central in the youths' analysis of enmity constructions where they argued disengaged citizenship and systems of exclusion were primary causes of constructions of the *dehumanized other*. The youth argued that the lack of inclusion and relations, as well as our limited exploration of relationality, shapes how we learn violence. The youth also argued normalized cultures of violence, for example learning racism within the home, learning identity differences equal deficiency or danger, and cultures of competition and rivalry, all contribute to the understanding and acceptance of violence. Consequently, peace pedagogies that neglect to recognize relationality often result in individualistically focused pedagogies that fail to appreciate the interconnections of the social world and the complexities of violence. In this regard, the youth suggested that through critical reflection, shared learning, and recognition of the socialization process maintaining cultures of violence, we begin to deeply analyze the normalizations of violence, including explorations of the invisible powers operating to maintain violence. Through this process alternatives to violence and the recognition of shared responsibilities for creating peaceful communities may also be envisioned.

Our analyses of violence (or enmity) began in the everyday lives of the youth participants, where relational ways of knowing and being were centered (i.e. using the methods of journaling and photography to analyze their everyday lives), and then expanded to explore the larger sociological influences of society, including how individuals are embedded within these social relations. In this regard Thayer-Bacon (2003) argues,

> We begin to understand that while starting an exploration of relationality from the micro level of personal relations helps us understand how we are intimately connected to others and highlights the primacy of interpersonal relations, we quickly come face-to-face with the public, social effects on that private relation at a macro level. The boundaries between private relations and social ones begin to dissolve. (p. 79)

It is within these interconnected micro and macro spaces where a relational epistemology can advance our understanding of violence toward building cultures of peace.

Within the proposed relational approach to violence transformation and peacebuilding in adult education, I argue for the privileging of three pedagogical strategies: (1) power analyses (of violence), incorporating the referential dimension of relational epistemologies whereby meaning and assumptions are deconstructed; (2) a sociological analysis of learning violence where the multiple and interconnected dimensions of violence are explored (including unlearning violence); and (3) the use of participatory education and engaged pedagogy.

2.1 *Deconstructing Violence through Explicit Power Analysis and Dialogue*

Exploring "how issues of power are tied to the legitimacy of knowledge" is fundamental to critical adult education theory (Huber, 2009, p. 641). In order to transform violence, learners must engage with the different conceptualizations of power and the assumptions embedded within them. Thayer-Bacon (2010) stresses the importance of exploring these assumptions within a relational epistemology to uncover the complexities of relations of power. Power assumptions influence adult education research and practice, and thus, it is essential to name power assumptions as well as the underlying theoretical frameworks guiding adult education, including education focused on peacebuilding. Yet, understanding the varying conceptions of power is not typically part of pedagogical practice or learner dialogue. In fact, Mei (PI) stated, "we don't talk about power" in reference to teaching and learning about peace and violence. Mei's statement was supported by the youth participants who shared they had never explicitly studied the varying conceptualizations of power (including the accompanying assumptions).

2.1.1 Power assumptions youth perspectives

It is essential to understand how the youth participants saw power operating, both as individuals and as an educational team, in order to explore how power influences constructions of enmity and to conceptualize and create strategies for building peace. For example, Audrey argued, "we don't really talk about the enemy. We talk about processes to bring peace." This statement led to a larger discussion about the focus of peacebuilding education and the complexities of power within the maintenance of cultures of violence and cultures of peace. During our critical dialogue, the youth participants mostly identified with an agent-centered power lens, describing visible and hidden forms of power, while at the same time blurring agency and structure. For example, Kira suggested power operates within and among actors. Yet, among the diverse strategies she recommended, the one she identified as being key to transforming violence was structurally based, emphasizing the importance of understanding how structures impact choice and action. Kira regularly referenced the importance of exposing how racism is hidden and systemic within Canadian refugee policy, resulting in certain groups of people having access to services and supports, while others are denied. Kira emphasized how systemic racism is deeply rooted within our constructions of the negative or dangerous other and expressed a need to further reflect on her assumptions of power in order to create strategies for change.

It is important to recognize that during our collaborative learning process, the participants' assumptions and definitions of power often changed, speaking to their continual formation, as well as the influence of collaborative learning. For instance, as we moved forward in the research process to begin to discuss strategies for peacebuilding, the participants shifted from the conceptual model of the *power cube* (spaces, levels, and forms of power) to embrace the *expressions of power* as argued by Veneklausen and Miller (2002). The youth engaged with the *power cube* to name the (interconnected) forms of power rooted in violence, then drew on *expressions of power* as they began to develop their pedagogies for peace. For example, during our analysis of enmity constructions, Opal discussed visible and hidden power, such as homophobia embedded within public discourse; however when exploring strategies for change, she regularly referred to *power with* strategies, emphasizing process and respectful relations as key to teaching for and building cultures of peace.

Table 10.1 demonstrates the youth's initial understandings of power as well as their proposed strategies for change.

The participants revealed that prior to this research, they had never explicitly considered how they developed their understanding of power, including assumptions, and how these assumptions influence social action and educational practice. Within a relational epistemology, understanding how we construct knowledge is essential (referential dimension). In this regard, Ross Howard (2000) suggests,

> All practice is grounded in beliefs about the nature of social, political and psychological reality. These core beliefs, which explain why and how practitioners expect to produce their intended effects, are more often implicit than explicit. Making them explicit permits us to identify the core assumptions of specific theories of practice, to articulate indicators which could help us evaluate if given theories are correct, and to revise

TABLE 10.1 Power assumptions and strategies for change – youth perspectives

Youth participant	How power operates	Strategies for change
Ziko	Agency power as influence	Avoid generalizations & challenge polarized stories.
Opal	Agency power as resistance	Importance of creating safe spaces. Work together to overcome differences. Importance of inclusion and engaging with others. Understand the roots of conflict.
Audrey	Power relations power as love	Importance of creating safe spaces. Work together to overcome differences.
Isla	Agency & relations	Challenge stereotypes.
Lily	Agency power as possession zero sum	Teaching about peace and violence needs to be extensive. Connect local and global issues.
Amya	Social structure & agency power as dominance	Teaching diverse perspectives.
Crystal	Agency power as dominance	Challenge popular culture normalizations of violence. Teaching diverse perspectives. Importance of creating safe spaces. Broad understandings of local and global issues.
Rachel	Agency	Importance of inclusion and engaging with others. Individuals are responsible for change. Education and information lead to action.
Kira	Agency power is owned & used	Teaching diverse perspectives. Understand the roots of conflict. Importance of inclusion and engaging with others. Challenge discriminatory or dehumanizing actions. Need to understand structural violence.
Dexie	Social structure power shapes communication	Reveal how structures influence choice and action.

practice if the core assumptions on which it is based are found to be imprecise or unwarranted. (p. 1007)

The discussions in Chapter 8 as well as Table 6.1, demonstrates the interrelationship and contradictions between power assumptions, power concepts, and strategies for change as well as the influence of these diverse perspectives informing social action. Our critical reflections and collective dialogue highlight the role for relational ways of knowing, particularly in regard to the participants multiple and often contradictory understandings of power. These analyses allowed the participants to reflect on their understandings of power and to investigate how their assumptions connected to (or contradicted) their peace praxis. During these analyses it became clear that explicit understandings of power, including the relations of power within our educational team, was an essential part of the process. These analyses also revealed how violence is internalized within society and the difficulties in recognizing *invisible* forms of power that deliberately operate to escape detection.

This research study was about naming and challenging patterns of violence, including the power embedded within violence, *with* youth for the purpose of building peace. This study demonstrated that explicit power analyses are essential toward the development of *critical consciousness* to make visible, the hidden and deep-rooted power operations and power relations contributing to normalizations of violence. This study also demonstrated that changes in construct occurred among the youth participants who began to see structural and cultural violence where they had not seen it before, and in forms that they had not considered. While both structural and agency lenses enhance our understanding of power in relation to learning enmity, a more comprehensive approach that incorporates both and additional frameworks, such as Foucault's (2000) power relations are necessary for the complexity of contemporary violence. Teaching about power assumptions and the multiple understandings of power may support a deeper level analysis of violence within our everyday lives, exposing the relations of power and the ontology of violence. By exploring power from multiple frameworks, the process of exposing invisible powers supporting a culture of violence and invisible powers supporting cultures of peace can be realized.

2.2   *Critical Adult Education: Unlearning Violence*

The WHO (2014) argue that focusing on "the nature and extent of violence, the populations at risk and the causes and consequences of violence are essential to developing well-informed national plans of action and policies, programmes and services to prevent and respond to violence" (p. 20). While this is all important, and true, focusing on the impact overlooks a critique of violence itself and the power mechanisms maintaining violence. Understanding power as discursive and fluid, and considering the impact of relations and norms on actions, provides a more comprehensive basis from which to develop ways of enhancing learning, envisioning, and creating a new way of conceptualizing conflict. Analyzing violence from this perspective, enables the study to include the *who* in the story (actors), the social systems and patterns which maintain violence (structure), and to explore how the stories (of enmity in this case) have become rooted in our everyday lives and rooted within our everyday interactions (norms and relations).

Understanding how we come to know and which knowledge is privileged, for which reason and for whose benefit, are fundamental questions within critical adult education. In fact, Brookfield (2005) argues a critical approach to adult learning involves many tasks, "such as learning how to perceive and challenge dominant ideology, unmask power, contest hegemony, overcome alienation, pursue liberation, reclaim reason, and practice democracy" (p. 2). Within a relational epistemology, this exploration of the structural dimension involves a focus on the organization of learning whereby multiple and interconnected elements of learning violence are explored. In this context, learning, knowledge, power, and process are bound together in an evolving sphere, requiring deliberate deconstructions to expose hidden and invisible mechanisms maintaining violence.

Learning to identify a person, a region, or a culture as (negatively) different or dangerous, involves the operation of deep-rooted and invisible power, including processes designed and performed to maintain inequitable relations, systems and structures. In this regard, Brookfield (2009) argues "the ideas and practices of hegemony become part and parcel of everyday life – the stock opinions, conventional wisdoms or common sense ways of seeing and ordering the world that people take for granted. If there is a conspiracy here, it is the conspiracy of the normal" (p. 301). Hayward (2013) further argues that inclusions and exclusions are normalized, materialized and "codified" within institutions, developing through "performances" which create expectations or social rules regarding identity and social action. Therefore, to question "the conspiracy of the normal" comes with risk. Questioning deeply penetrated normalizations of violence within a critical analysis also comes with the risk of failing to recognize the fluidity of perspectives, changing contexts, and risks the "metanarrative of social justice" (Sidorkin, 2002, p. 177). Thus, bridging critical and post-structural analyses is important, where "pluralism and critique of the Western canon, on the one hand, peacefully coexists with adherence to critical theory with its liberatory metanarratives and claims of universal justice on the other" (Sidorkin, 2002, p. 174). Sidorkin (2002) argues it is possible to embrace both theoretical positions so long as the complexities are acknowledged and continuously part of the dialogue.

Freire (2003), Brookfield (2005), and Wink (2011) caution about the indoctrination involved in many forms of education, supporting the youths' concerns about the role of formal education in maintaining negative constructions of other. In order to critique violence, particularly embedded and unquestioned violence, Freire (1970, 2003) argued for the development of *critical consciousness* as a means to empower those oppressed by hegemonic socializations, and to create social change towards equitable living (or cultures of peace). Chovanec and Lange (2007) suggest *critical consciousness* is "a process by which humans, as knowing subjects, achieve a deepened awareness of the socio-cultural reality that shapes their lives and their capacity to transform that reality" (p. 133). In this regard, Freire (1970) calls on educators to engage in empowerment education to support people, particularly marginalized people, to expose structural violence and create strategies for change. Critical education, including empowerment education, is essential for peacebuilding considering the pervasive normalization of violence (Carter, 2010).

The development of a critical consciousness also requires a post-structural analysis where the utopian *truth* is challenged and where power relations between teachers and learners, as well as among learners are continuously analyzed. In fact Sidorkin (2002) argues the very nature of teaching and learning includes power inequities. Wright (2000) reminds "those of us attempting to undertake progressive praxis to continually reflect on how power operates within and among the discourse of empowerment" (p. 138). In this regard, Weiler (1988) argues for a critical pedagogy where subjectivities are encouraged, respected, and valued, speaking to the "competing subjectivities of teacher and students" (p. 148). While, Sidorkin and Weiler are working from a schooling perspective, as well as a child-adult educational relationship, they share concerns and critiques with adult educators such as Ellsworth. Pedagogically, the development of *critical consciousness,* requires explicit power analyses and critical, collaborative dialogue.

Francis (2002) argues "conflict can be defined as the friction caused by difference, proximity and movement. Since people and their lives are, fortunately, not identical, isolated or static, conflict between them is inevitable: a sign of life" (p. 3). Exploring how to create pedagogies for peace are necessarily grounded in an appreciation for the possibilities nested within conflict. Freire (2004) similarly claimed that peace is not the absence of conflict, but rather "the struggle for fairly and critically confronting conflicts" (p. 118). In this regard, Sidorkin (2002) challenges educators to engage in dialogue with *evil*, with those whom are (or appear to be) holding opposing ideologies and values. He describes dialogue between racialized persons and "skinheads" as an example of where dialogue is truly needed, while also acknowledging the difficulty with engaging in a dialogic process with those who are uninterested in dialogue/ change (Sidorkin, 2002). Thus, building peace (while *unlearning* violence) requires an appreciation for difference, respect for diverse perspectives, and sustained critical reflection where power is explicitly explored, even when the dialogue is with *the enemy*.

Transforming violence is a complex process requiring an interdisciplinary analysis and the merging of multiple frameworks. The complexity of this task is further challenged as peace work within adult education is under theorized, lacking ontological and epistemological discussion and development. Diverse theories of change in relation to violence transformation exist, ranging from community (such as community development theory) to political and cultural shifts (such as critical theories or social justice theories). In relation to cultural or norm-based theories of change, the WHO (2014) claim there is value in social and cultural norm change strategies to reduce violence, however evaluations of effectiveness and impact are lacking resulting in limited uptake in most contexts; thus, identifying a gap in adult education research and practice.

Each theoretical framework designed to transform violence comes with embedded assumptions. These assumptions about why and how conflict occurs influences the strategies we employ to transform conflict and violence (Keashly & Warters, 2000). Similarly, how we come to know and understand *peace* is an important part of the overall theoretical framework for creating cultures of peace. Galtung (1996) argues "peace studies demands an epistemology that sees the world as flexible, and that produces equally flexible images of that world" seemingly arguing for a post-structural analyses (p. 22). Galtung (2006) further argues there are three potential peace epistemologies: empirical, critical and constructive. Each of these epistemologies represent a structural dimension, or an organization of how we learn peace (and unlearn violence).

Several of the youth participants privileged an empirical peace epistemology, or the process of applying lessons from the past to the future, where data is used to "reveal patterns and conditions for peace" (Galtung, 1996, p. 9). For instance, participants focused on conflict mapping and assessing the root causes of a conflict, as important processes for creating new theories for peace. Galtung (1996) argued that an empirical peace epistemology focuses on investigating what has occurred in relation to violence and peace, so that "the observed becomes foreseen and the unforeseen unobserved" (p. 11). Traditional peacebuilding, as described in Chapter 4, falls within an empirical approach, where information gathered "reveals" opportunities or theories for creating peace (Table 10.2). Contemporary peacebuilding education extends beyond the data collection and conflict analysis processes to explore deeper structural causes of violence and the relations of power embedded in these processes. Peacebuilding education offers additional perspectives about the importance of relational epistemologies. Specifically, peacebuilding education is grounded in relations where the focus is less on fixing conflict (conflict resolution) and instead on transforming conflict toward social change (conflict transformation).

Critical peace epistemologies focus on a critique of systems and structures, which create and maintain peacelessness (Galtung, 1996). Galtung (1996) argued the "logic of criticism is to adjust reality so that the future will produce data with the observed being the desired and the rejected being unobserved" (p. 11). Otherwise, the preferred reality becomes real and the systems being critiqued or rejected are no longer functioning. Critical epistemologies stem from a good-bad, right-wrong duality, rooted in values (Galtung, 1996). The youth participants regularly focused on *good values* and *peace values* to critique systems and structures within society, while at the same time they challenged each other about who determines what is *good* and what is *peaceful*. For example, during the development of the theory of change, Rachel challenged her peers to consider who has the authority to decide what is *good* and *peaceful*. Overall, their critiques fall in line with traditional critical adult education approaches to peace work, or critical epistemology, where inequity is challenged in order to transform social injustices and relations toward adherence to peace values (Table 10.2). Critical adult education challenges ideology while bringing issues of voice, participation, and power to the center. Giroux's (1993) *pedagogy of representation*, as previously described in Chapter 4, provides an example of a critical technique to scrutinize how meanings and identities of *others* are constructed. Within this critical pedagogical approach, values and theories for change are centered. Building cultures of peace within adult education requires a push back to neoliberalism and the use of creative pedagogical and administrative practice to ensure peace work remains central, as it was in early adult education.

Finally, constructive epistemologies "takes the theories about what might work and brings them together with values about what ought to work … the logic of constructivism is to come up with new theories, adjusted to values so that the desired is foreseen and the rejected unforeseen" (Galtung, 1996, p. 11). International humanitarian law (IHL) is an example of a negative peace, constructive epistemology (Table 10.2). Treaty-based, legal instruments are based on the premise that guidelines for appropriate behaviour (values of what is acceptable) will shape action. In the case of IHL, rules named in the Geneva Conventions of 1949, including the additional protocols and evolving international law, stipulate appropriate and acceptable behaviour in armed conflict. However, the values embedded within IHL both compliment and contradict peace values. For instance, IHL shares with peace values a fundamental respect for humanity, however, violence is not always deterred in IHL. In fact, during armed conflict, combatants are legally allowed to kill an enemy combatant, within certain rules determining means and methods. IHL is a harm reduction approach to violence prevention that fails to critique violence itself, thus failing to prevent future escalations of violence (Greenberg Research, 1999; Fresard, 2004). In relation to IHL, the youth participants discussed the delicacy of creating a universal system of rules combined with an appreciation for diverse perspectives and experiences, embracing a critical, post-structural framework.

Table 10.2 provides a summary of the ontological, epistemological, assets, challenges, and peace strategies involved in: (1) peacebuilding, (2) international humanitarian law, and (3) critical adult education approaches for comparative purposes.

Ontologically, peacebuilding, international humanitarian law, and critical adult education all support an inevitability of conflict and share a common concern for respect for human dignity. Each approach differs epistemologically, due to varying emphasis on data, theories, and values. Nevertheless, merging the three approaches reveals possibilities for creating new theories, informed by data and values, to transform violence and build cultures of peace. Understanding the epistemological and ontological foundations of educational strategies for building cultures of peace is essential. Galtung (1996) argues for the privileging of constructive epistemologies, while embracing the learnings within empirical and constructive approaches, stating:

> If they had been empiricists only, they would have been content with empirical studies of caves and of the carrying capacity for human beings; if they had been criticisms only, they would have been content with declarations deploring the short comings of caves and humans. Constructivism transcends what empiricism reveals, and offers constructive proposals. Criticism is an indispensable bridge between the two. There has to be motivation, anchored in values. (p. 11)

Furthermore, Galtung and Tschudi (2002) argue that focusing on attitudinal change is a "liberal fallacy," focusing on behaviour change is a "conservative fallacy," and focusing on contradiction is a "Marxist fallacy"; instead, peace

TABLE 10.2　Alternative approaches to building cultures of peace

	Ontology	Epistemology	Assets	Challenges	Strategies
Peacebuilding *Peacebuilding education (includes additional features)*	Conflict is natural. Conflict is an opportunity for change. * Relations and connections.	*Empirical peace*: focus on data gathered during conflict assessment to develop theories for change. Emphasis on relations, interdependence, and human security.	Embrace conflict as opportunity for social change and transformation. Embraces both a positive peace lens, focusing on holistic approach to building sustainable and healthy relations as well as a negative peace lens, focusing on the impact of weapons of war.	Interdisciplinarity can increase challenges with practical implementation. Tensions (funding and otherwise) exist between human security and national security agendas. Acceptance of peace building approaches is diverse depending on the community context.	Conflict assessment Conflict Mapping * Non-violent communication * Peaceful processes * Inclusion * Youth & adult partnership

	Ontology	Epistemology	Assets	Challenges	Strategies
International humanitarian law	Violence is inevitable. Respect for human dignity is a universal goal.	*Constructive peace*: focus on the interconnections of theory (treaty based system to control behaviour) and values (human rights framework.) Legal frameworks enhance social control and reduce violence during armed conflict.	Harm reduction approach that seeks to mitigate violence during armed conflict, with a particular focus on those not engaged or no longer engaged in the armed conflict. Focus on respect for human dignity. The main legal framework, the Geneva Conventions of 1949, have been universally ratified.	Embedded within a militaristic framework that fails to address the roots of armed conflict or identify ways to build healthy relationships. Relatively unknown among general populations. IHL is only applicable during armed conflict.	Law development Treaty ratification Dissemination of the rules of law Judicial responses to violations of the law

TABLE 10.2　Alternative Approaches to Building Cultures of Peace (*cont.*)

	Ontology	Epistemology	Assets	Challenges	Strategies
Critical adult education	Social structures are unjustly constructed to maintain inequality. Inequities exist, particularly for those on the margins.	*Critical peace*: focus on relation between data and values. Challenge and create new ways of conceptualizing social structures and relations to reduce inequities. Diverse ways of knowing are embraced and encouraged.	Core focus on power and knowledge. Brings inequities and the marginalized to the centre raising questions about whose voice is being heard in social conflicts. Embraces ideological critique in diverse settings and challenges dominant ideologies. Historically rooted in community based education for adults with an emancipatory and social justice focus.	Places significant power in the hands of the educator which can encourage and sustain hegemonic ideologies and practices. Increasingly critiqued for contributing to the co-modification of education and is developing stronger connections to neo-liberal influences.	Analyze & critique popular culture. Critical self-reflection about identity. Naming & identifying spaces and forms of power in learning. Explicitly learning power. Exploring history. Critical thinking & critical literacy skills.

epistemologies need to incorporate all three (p. 153). Peace requires a comprehensive process that engages mind, body and soul, including the relational reality of self, others, and the whole of society.

2.3 Participatory Education & Engaged Pedagogy: Learning Peaceful Processes

Hart (2004) suggests, "if we want to educate young people so that they are capable of creating a culture of peace, we need to nourish mutual-respect, caring, and compassion in our relationships; we need to model what we hope to teach" (p. 113). Relations between teachers and learners, and between learners, are an integral part of educating for peaceful processes (Thayer-Bacon, 2003). Centering relationships, including exploring relations of power, provides an opportunity to transform societal responses to conflict (Lederach, 2006).

Our research methodology embraced PAR-inspired principles to engage youth in a process of exploring how power influences the constructions of enmity and how youth can participate in the creation of pedagogies for peace. PAR offers an alternative process to knowledge construction by emphasizing dialogue, relationships, and inclusivity (Manzo & Brightbill, 2007). In fact, Pain, Kesby, and Kindon (2007) argue it is "the connectedness and relationality of people, places and processes of participation that provide one of the most invigorating aspects of PAR's ability to effect meaningful change and political transformation" (p. 226). Within participatory processes, the emphasis moves beyond a transactional relational engagement (i.e. donating money to a charity) to include a transformational engagement where the interconnections among people and communities are valued and critically explored (MCIC, 2013).

A "pedagogy of relation claims that what we do in education is less important than the sort of relations we develop" (Sidorkin, 2002, p. 197). Within a relational pedagogy, Sidorkin (2002) argues that relationism, unlike relativism, requires accountability and responsibility beyond one's actions to consider one's actions in relation to others. Similarly, hooks (2010) argues engaged pedagogy "assumes that every student has a valuable contribution to make to the learning process. However, it does not assume that all voices should occupy the same amount of time," demonstrating the complexities of engaged pedagogy, participation and relations of power (p. 21). Thus, participation, dialogue, empowerment, and action were key aspects of this participatory research process and key aspects to relational epistemology.

2.3.1 Representationalism and participation

Participatory and collaborative learning was fundamental to this research. As described in Chapter 6, this study employed a PAR-inspired methodology, embracing the principles of inclusion, participation, dialogue, action, social change, and empowerment. This methodological approach was selected to create space for, and to honour the perspectives of youth in relation to their understandings of violence and their capacity to create pedagogies for peace. Centering the voices and perspectives of the youth participants was a delicate process and required a commitment to continuous reflexivity. Although this research study in some ways did not respect the principles of orthodox PAR (the research question was pre-selected, for example), respecting the voices and decisions of the participants, and engaging in collective empowerment remained the primary focus.

Shor (1992) argued that empowering education (in this case empowering research) is fraught with "hope, humor, setbacks, breakthroughs, and creative life, on a long and winding road paved with dreams whose time is overdue" (p. 263). This experience has exposed the possibilities ("hope") and complexities ("setbacks") within empowerment and participatory education/ research, particularly in relation to participant voice and the role of the researcher to share their perspectives broadly. Beyond continuous check-ins with the participants, choosing when and how to analyze and share the youths' perspectives, required a high level of ethical consideration and critical reflection. Negotiating an analytical process that was both participant driven, as well as researcher driven (as required for the doctoral process) was a delicate operation. This experience has enhanced my understanding of participatory processes, especially with youth, and will allow me to build on the social analysis provided by the 10 young adult participants to engage in future PAR research around violence transformation.

2.3.2   Youth as peace builders

Violence and peace are interconnected in the lives of youth, both directly and indirectly. As adult educators, our failure to engage youth as full participants in peacebuilding comes with great risk. For example, Mei argues adults are not skilled in recognizing or knowing "how to ask the questions to get that information [information about violence and personal safety] out of the kids, in order to keep them safe." Mei further argues, "Normalization of violence does not just sit on kid's shoulders, it sits on adult shoulders and we need to work with them to start taking responsibility for keeping kids safe." This caution was animated by an EWHL guest speaker, William Tarr who described the rehabilitation failings for child soldiers in Sierra Leone due to the lack of recognition of the power relations between youth, and between adults working with youth (personal communication, October 17, 2013). Mr. Tarr described how "there was no support for the Commanders [of child soldiers]; and lots of children still had loyalty to the commanders" (personal communication, October 17, 2013). Mr. Tarr's example highlights how relations of power between youth and between youth and adults must be considered in the pursuit of peace (Orsini, 2010).

Youth bring abilities and capacities to peace work that are similar to their adult counterparts. They also bring unique experiences and abilities to pursue alternative approaches to peace. Nabavi and Lund (2010) argue that youth are more creative, thrive in learning in fast pace environments, and are highly equipped in mobilizing others for change. Linds and Goulet (2010) argue, "the role of the adult is to exercise trust in the youth: to believe that youth are the ones who know their reality best" (p. 237). While reflecting on the abilities of youth as peace builders, and youth within peacebuilding teams, PI Chester shared:

> One thing that I have always appreciated about youth is that they push the boundaries of thinking. You know, we as adults, particularly for people of my generation, we have a framework within which we are very comfortable operating but the youth have a different framework. We ignore that at our risk because youth tend to be more adventuresome and more curious and so allow them to expand that curiosity in ways that allow them to explore. It's like a voyage of exploration because they discover, and through discovery they learn.

The youth participants' explorations around the use of social media, for example, illustrate their ability to push educational boundaries and opportunities for change. The use of technology in peace work in adult education, for example the use of Twitter during the Arab Spring movement, reveals emerging pedagogical processes and new educational spaces for peace work that is largely being pursued and created by youth. For example, during the Arab Spring, an Egyptian Canadian member of the EWHL working group, regularly shared live streaming of events in Cairo. Connecting with youth who were actively engaged in the Arab Spring, in Cairo, in real time, brought new learning and teaching possibilities to our local work in Halifax, Nova Scotia. While the use of technology as a new pedagogical tool is not solely utilized by youth, young people are leading innovations in this area. Given the increasing influence of globalization and resulting technological developments, including many youths' utility with rapidly changing technologies, it is essential that adult educators engage youth as learners and teachers in the pursuit of cultures of peace, to ensure a fuller and more informed picture of our social context is considered.

3 Critical, Constructive and Relational Pedagogies for Peace

Thayer-Bacon (2003) argues that due to our "social embeddedness" our ability to *know* must be informed by multiple perspectives and multiple theoretical frameworks. Therefore, thoughtfully merging a relational epistemology with Galtung's (1996) peace epistemologies, honours the relational ways of knowing within society, including the referential and structural dimensions of relational epistemologies. In this way, epistemology must consider *subjects* as "social beings living in-relation-with others. Epistemology must be redefined so that it can be sensitive to actual outcomes, and require awareness of diverse contexts" (Thayer-Bacon, 2003, p. 34).

Within our analytical and collective critique of constructions of violence, a relational epistemology became evident among the youth who began to see violence and opportunities to build peace with new perspectives and collective synergy. Our incorporation of critical self-reflection and collaborative dialogue animated how our individual and collective theories of knowledge were embedded in relational ways of knowing, and deeply intertwined as social constructions. Thus, merging the relationship building and conflict transformation focus of peacebuilding with the treaty-based, harm reduction aims of international humanitarian law, in combination with the ideological critiques of critical adult education, with a relational epistemological framework, may offer a comprehensive lens for disrupting violence and building cultures of peace.

During our research process, we utilized a critical education framework to deconstruct enmity and violence, by loosely following the methodological process located within Open Space for Dialogue and Enquiry (OSD&E) (Andreotti, 2011). As previously described, OSD&E is designed to reframe hegemonic knowledge production in a safe learning space were difference is embraced (Andreotti, 2011). OSD&E embraces multiple epistemological guidelines including: all knowledge is valid, partial, and incomplete (Andreotti, 2011). ODS&E utilizes a pedagogical model that flows from the creation of safe learning spaces, to individual critical reflection, to group dialogue, followed by explorations around collective social responsibility (Andreotti, 2011). ODS&E can be used in multiple sites for adult education, and is a particularly helpful pedagogical process to use when the learners are together for short-term educational experiences.

The importance of critical reflection and ideology critique, as understood within critical adult education and critical pedagogy, shined in the dialogue and the images shared by the youth participants as well as their planned strategies for change. Beyond the individual and collective critique of violence, relational ways of knowing emerged throughout our research in both explicit and implicit ways, emphasizing the complex interconnections between self and society in regard to knowledge and learning. In the following section, I highlight a modified version of the OSD&E pedagogical process, incorporating relationality as a pedagogical model for transforming violence.

OSD&E is designed for use within a collective learning experience. The first steps in OSD&E involve the use of an educational stimulus to spark individual reflection. In our research process, the youth engaged in critical reflection (using photography, journals, and reflective questions) to explore issues of knowledge construction generally, as well as constructions of enmity specifically, prior to coming together as a larger research group. Within these reflections, the youth identified how their social experiences contributed to their understandings of self, society, power, and violence (described in detail in Chapter 7). This was a theme that continued throughout the research process. Unlike OSD&E, where individual self-reflection occurs following a shared stimulus, the youth participants selected and/or created their own stimulus to consider enmity constructions and power.

After engaging in critical self-reflection, the youth participants came together for further critical dialogue focused on social action planning in the area of violence transformation. As part of this process, we developed *community standards* to support the creation of a safer learning space where difference was embraced, respectful dialogue was encouraged and practiced, and where participation and voice were centered. We used the epistemological framework of OSD&E as well as the contributions of the participants to support our collaborative learning. After exploring how enmity is constructed from multiple perspectives, the research team engaged in a planning process to create strategies for transforming violence.

While the closure of the Canadian Red Cross educational programming greatly impacted the youths' ability to revise and/or create peace pedagogies, the theory of change they developed (as described in Chapter 9) can serve as a tool for future programming, within the Canadian Red Cross as well as within the lives of the youth as they continue to engage in peacebuilding work. In relation to the action element within PAR, Stuttaford and Coe (2007) claim that social action does not always happen immediately (or at all), nor is the action element always successful, however, it is important to recognize that the "learning may not lead to action in the place it is learn[ed]" but it may contribute to future action nonetheless (p. 193). Stuttaford's and Coe's assertion rings true for this research process. For instance, I have heard from several participants since the conclusion of our research study, who shared how they have continued to use some of the pedagogical tools we used together to explore issues of peace and violence, how they continue to challenge constructions of enmity within their family/communities, and how they are

TABLE 10.3 Pedagogical processes – critical, constructive & relational adult education

Pedagogical process	Open space for dialogue & enquiry (Andreotti, 2011)	Transforming violence together (Research pedagogical process)	Commentary
#1	Safe space (setting the learning rules; epistemological basis)	Self-assessment (explore assumptions, bias, world views, power influences through photography, journaling, and critical self-reflective questions)	Prior to connecting as a group, the youth participants engaged in critical self-reflections individually, considering how knowledge is constructed generally and how their world views shape *truth(s)*.
#2	Stimulus (use of stimulus for critical thinking)	Conflict assessment – individual (explore what fuels and challenges constructions of enmity; explicit focus on power influences)	The youth selected and/or created their own stimulus (from their own everyday experiences) to engage in critical self-reflection around violence and power.
#3	Reflexive questions (individual self-reflection)	Creating safer spaces (develop rules, practice democratic processes, and naming and reflect on power within group)	In congruence with our PAR-inspired methodology, we focused heavily on creating safer learning spaces for our research by developing community standards together, by exploring the relations of power within our research group, and by using peaceful processes to engage in the research process.

Pedagogical process	Open space for dialogue & enquiry (Andreotti, 2011)	Transforming violence together (Research pedagogical process)	Commentary
#4	Group dialogue (identifying diverse perspectives)	Conflict assessment – collective (group dialogue and critical reflection; exploring diverse perspectives)	We used empirically based tools from peace building (ex. Power Cube, Onion, Force Field Analysis) to analyze violence; we further explored the theories embedded within a legal approach to peace work, specifically discussing IHL (ex. Geneva Conventions and RC/RC principles) to explore values; and from critical adult education, we used Giroux's pedagogy of representation to challenge how violence is learned and opportunities for unlearning violence.
#5	Strategies for change (action and collective responsibility)	Develop theory of change – collective (strategies for disrupting violence and building peace)	Based on a relational epistemology, the youth created a theory of change for building cultures of peace. Relationality was centered during this process.

TABLE 10.3 Pedagogical processes – critical, constructive & relational adult education (*cont.*)

Pedagogical process	Open space for dialogue & enquiry (Andreotti, 2011)	Transforming violence together (Research pedagogical process)	Commentary
#6		Design & plan	We were in this stage of the pedagogical process when the Canadian Red Cross funding was abruptly cancelled. The youth were planning to revise and create new pedagogical tools and a new methodology for the EWHL working group to engage other youth in violence transformation.
#7		Monitor & evaluation	We loosely identified indicators for cultures of peace hoping that we could re-visit our work at a future date.

in the process of pursuing additional formal education in peace studies as a result of our research together.

Table 10.3 highlights a brief overview of the pedagogical process of Open Space for Dialogue and Enquiry and the modified processes that we followed in our critical exploration of violence, incorporating empirical, critical, constructive and relational epistemologies. It is important to note that while this table presents the process as linear, and to a certain extent it was, the learning cycle was much more complicated, cyclical, and interconnected.

Galtung (1996) argues "creating peace obviously has to do with reducing violence (cure) and avoiding violence (prevention)" (p. 2). Galtung, also argued that in order to achieve peace, we need a "do-able" theory. Thus, after facilitating the research process with the youth, and collectively developing a theory of change for building cultures of peace, I developed an overarching pedagogical process for disrupting constructions of enmity and pursing peace within critical adult education (outlined in Table 10.3). The proposed process provides a pedagogical tool to disrupt patterns of violence and to build cultures of peace with youth, while privileging relationality.

To represent the interconnections of the proposed pedagogical process for transforming violence as outlined in Table 10.3, I have included an illustration, modeling the potential for violence transformation within adult education (Figure 10.1). Safer learning spaces, critical reflection, and collaborative learning frame the pedagogical process for disrupting violence and creating peace. Exploring enmity constructions from a direct, structural and cultural perspective, in combination with considering the mechanisms of power influencing these constructions (visible, hidden, and invisible) sits as a prime area for deep critical reflection, including individual and collaborative critical reflection (referential dimension of relational epistemology). Exploring peace epistemologies (empirical, critical, constructive, and relational) are another key area of focus within a pedagogical process for peace (structural dimension of relational epistemologies). Naming the epistemological basis underlying a pedagogical

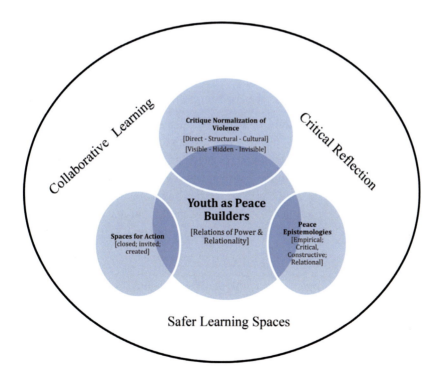

FIGURE 10.1   Challenging the ontology of violence

process is essential to explore peace and violence. Finally, identifying potential sites for peace-focused, adult learning within closed, invited, or created spaces as described by Gaventa (2006), are key to violence transformation. Embedded within this overall process are the relations of power that exist within the group, and participatory process based on engaged pedagogy.

This pedagogical model may serve as an educational tool to name how violence interpenetrates our lives in multiple ways and in multiple spaces, from micro to macro levels, from direct to cultural types, and from visible to invisible forms; as well as to name how knowledge (i.e. understandings of power) is conceived and evaluated. Within this study, the youth demonstrated how *critical consciousness* can be facilitated through deep critical self-reflection and enhanced within collaborative learning where diverse perspectives are shared and valued. Harris (2008) argues that critical educators are able to reduce "tendencies to violence by increasing people's capacity for critical reflection and thus equipping them to analyze, and potentially resist, future calls to violence" (p. 38). Within teaching for the development of a *critical consciousness,* is a call for action while centering issues of power and opportunities for social change. I further argue for the incorporation of a relational epistemology to expose the relations of power and relational ways of knowing that are embedded within knowledge construction.

4   Experiential Learning

The youth emphasized the role of experiential learning as a pedagogical tool to transform violence and develop peaceful practices, and as a means to support enhanced awareness, increased engagement and the development of respectful relations. Galtung (1996b), also argued experiential learning was an effective means to build empathy and understanding, two key values in peace work. Freire (2005) emphasized the value of experiential learning to create depth in perspective and to consider strategies for change. Similarly, Francis (2002) argued

> Experiential learning is a strong thread in my account, in which common themes and values emerge as well as points of tension and difference. It also illustrates and discusses issues of co-facilitation and the role of facilitators, their exercise of power and responsibility, the pressures experienced by facilitators and the kinds of decisions they have to take in response to changing demands and moods within the group, and the changing dynamics, roles and power relations it embodies. (p. 132)

While experiential learning was not an explicit focus of this research process, it is an unexpected learning that emerged from the youths' work exploring sites and pedagogies for peace and an area requiring further research.

5 Sites for Peace Work within Adult Education

Peace and conflict education occurs in many spaces, with children, youth, and adults. Exploring how peace sites and pedagogies can be created to challenge constructions of enmity requires a careful analysis of possible spaces and the powers embedded in these spaces. Gaventa's (2006) *Power Cube* offers a useful framework to consider spaces for peace work. Gaventa (2006) organizes spaces for transformation into three areas: closed, invited, and created. Closed spaces are not accessible to everyone, and particularly inaccessible to those most affected by social issues, in this case violence (for example, government policy development). Invited spaces are spaces where actors and organizations are invited to participate, but the participation comes with conditions (for example, invitation to a government roundtable when the policy is already written). Finally, created spaces are the spaces that citizens can develop, perhaps outside of the typical forums for exploring change. As the youth and I approached consideration of spaces for peace work, the funding for their community education work was cut. Therefore, we did not identify specific learning sites or spaces, however we added consideration to our overall framework for where peace work can and should be taking place. The closure of the program and resulting shift in our analyses was troubling for the youth participants who were keen to take action with their new framework exploring violence transformation. Father Tompkins of the Antigonish Movement famously stated, "Ideas have to have feet" and this shortcoming of this research project was certainly felt wholeheartedly by all those involved.

6 Critical Adult Education and Violence Transformation: Concluding Thoughts

Adult education that neglects to challenge normalizations of violence, and the relations that maintain violence as an accepted norm in society, further reinforces unquestioned ideologies of the dehumanized other. Failing to uproot the *hidden* and *invisible* processes that maintain violence, can lead to sustained dehumanization and enmity constructions. The youth I had the privilege of learning with, highlighted multiple processes in play contributing to their own and their peers' constructions of enmity over time. The youth participants also shared experiences and reflections about processes used to disrupt hegemony as well as the challenges of transforming hegemony – particularly as a group outside of many political arenas.

Within this critical, collaborative, and participatory methodology, the youth revealed *hidden* and in some cases began to reveal *invisible* power mechanisms maintaining violence in their everyday lives. They also created a thoughtful theory of change for building cultures of peace, based on their analysis of the multiple data sets we gathered, analyzed, and synthesized, including the emerging questions we shared and discussed along the way. Following the data analysis, the youth agreed the combination of awareness, engagement, and respectful relations were essential to building cultures of peace.

The first two sections of this chapter speak to the critical awareness piece of this work (i.e. exploring power explicitly and through dialogue; and challenging the ontology of violence through critical adult education pedagogical processes). In relation to engaged learners, the youth participants' insights were discussed in detail in Chapters 7 and 8, as they debated whether *informed* or *engaged* people should be the priority for educational processes for peace. In the end, the youth argued awareness/informed and engaged are not separate entities to consider in the process of building peace. In fact Opal referenced the work of bell hooks (2010) to validate this point. hooks (2010) stated: "expanding both heart and mind, engaged pedagogy makes us better learners because it asks us to embrace and explore the practice of knowing together, to see intelligence as a resource that can strengthen our common good" (p. 22). Similarly, Galtung (1983) argued that peace-related education needs to go beyond awareness, or exploring the causes and consequences of violence to include action to change and/or transform it. The youth participants identified the importance of modeling peaceful relations and practices to support both the engagement of, and increased understanding of learners, in peace work for the purpose of social change.

The quintessential elements of critical adult education are challenging unquestioned assumptions and acting for social change. A critical pedagogical approach to violence transformation which draws upon the work of Freire, Galtung, and Thayer-Bacon, aims to challenge hegemonic and violent constructions of other, while focusing on transformation through intentional education and learning processes grounded in relations. Educational interventions framed within a relational epistemology and ontology, center a sociological analysis of *learning* violence, and thus, highlight opportunities for *unlearning* violence.

CHAPTER 11

Peace, Pedagogy and Possibilities

> This work is often difficult because sometimes you feel like you are not getting a lot of support from institutions or society at large. Of course in a way if it wasn't difficult it would already be done. If there weren't difficult, on-going, compelling, human issues then there would be no need for us to be engaging people to think about peace and conflict and empathy and power and global citizenship. But that's the world. That's the world that we're in.
> NING (PROFESSIONAL INFORMANT)

∴

I remember as a child hearing the story of children in a community who were at risk of falling off a high cliff (to my knowledge this was a fictitious story). In this story, children were dying or being injured after falling and thus, the community responded by placing ambulances at the base of the cliff to provide immediate medical attention. The story continues to describe how the community realized they could save more children if a fence was built around the perimeter of the cliff. But what if children falling was not the full *diagnosis*? And what if ambulances and fences were not the most effective *therapies*? Galtung (1996) argues there is futility in applying the medical model, *diagnosis – prognosis – therapy*, to the analysis of violence. How we identify the problem (*diagnosis*) impacts how we respond (*therapy*), and ultimately impacts the prediction or proposed outcome (*prognosis*) (Galtung, 1996). In relation to violence, we provide many *ambulances* to respond to the impacts, and we build a few *fences* along the way to reduce violence, but rarely do we question violence itself. The majority of social analyses on violence focus on violence reduction and prevention, not transforming normalizations of violence. The majority of social analyses on violence also exclude the voices of youth.

This research was focused on an analysis of the *problem* – the normalizations and internalized acceptance of violence; and potential educational *therapies* – explorations of pedagogical strategies for violence transformation. The purpose of this study was to examine *with* Canadian young adults, how violence (i.e. dehumanized constructions of other, or *enmity*) can be reduced, prevented, and transformed through education, toward building cultures of peace. The 10 young adults involved in this critical, collaborative qualitative study highlighted a multitude of spaces where violence is embedded within their everyday lives, and within youth cultures generally. We endeavoured to investigate both thinking and action to consider possible peace praxis. Learning *with* young adults was fundamental to this research. By exploring violence, power, and peacebuilding together, this study revealed peacebuilding pedagogies within critical adult education and raised important questions about the significance of relationally based peacebuilding. Our findings highlight:

1. the *role for critical adult education* "including critical pedagogy" in questioning normalizations of violence and making visible, the *hidden* and *invisible* powers which work to maintain violence, in order to disrupt patterns of violence. The youth specifically identified the following influences in the construction of enmity that require explicit power analyses and critique: identity differences viewed as deficient, disengaged citizenship/relations, systems of exclusion, normalizations of violence, and competition and rivalry;
2. the *risks associated with neglecting to include youth* in adult education research and practice, including limited insight into the everyday lives of youth and the forms of power that interpenetrate youth cultures. The risks include the development of flawed theories and practice that contradict the learner-centered principles of adult education;
3. the *benefits of collaborative and participatory learning*, including an appreciation for diverse perspectives, plural realities, and difference (i.e. conflict) as beneficial, as well as a recognition of the skills and abilities of young adults to create social change;
4. finally, the importance of re-connecting peace work and the field of adult education, where *respectful and equitable relations* and *relationality* are centered and *relationally based peacebuilding* are aspired for.

This research shows how explicit power analyses, and collective and participatory learning processes, framed within critical adult education, can create space for dialogue and action toward building cultures of peace. This study also reveals the role of youth in identifying forms of violence as well as being capable and integral agents for social change. Our findings contribute to the literature on critical adult education, youth engagement, peace and violence, as well as peacebuilding education.

1 Research Significance

Violence is embedded in our everyday lives, steeped in symbols, language, behaviors, and deep-rooted *cultural violence*. Popular culture, formal schooling, family and friends, all shape how identity is formed, often within a framework of difference as deficient. Within the context of contemporary violence, the politics of fear and the construction of enmity is thriving in Canada. Canadians can simply turn on the television or read the local news to *learn* who the enemy is today. Whether it is youth because of the planned actions of the "murderous misfits!" involved in the Halifax Valentine's Day plot (Auld & Tutton, 2015); or a woman who wears a niqab in court, a practice Stephen Harper called "anti-women" (Chase, 2015), the enemy is vividly and publicly constructed. Unfortunately, rarely do we question who is telling the story of enmity, the motivation for the angle of the story, or the violence embedded (*hidden* and *invisible*) in the story.

In fact, Canadians have participated in a politics of fear that has endured throughout history, focusing in some cases on new *threats* (for example, Muslim women) while consistently maintaining difference as deficient or *dangerous* for persistently marginalized groups (for example, Indigenous peoples). The example of Japanese Canadians being detained by the thousands during the Second World War, is a glaring animation of how the story of an enemy is constructed and acted upon in our society. According to MacKenzie King, Canadians of Japanese heritage, many of whom had lived in Canada for multiple generations, were deemed a threat to Canadian security due to their heritage. The deep-rooted racism underpinning this enmity construction, was acknowledged in 1988 by Brian Mulroney, who formally apologized to those detained on behalf of the Government of Canada. How people learn to see difference as deficient, other as negative, and enemy as dehumanized, involves generations of socialization where fear and hate trump understanding and love.

Examining how violence evolves, often unquestioned, and how we are able to create a sense of *otherness* that dehumanizes and defines people as the enemy is important learning that should be embraced in all societies (Apple, 2011; ICRC, 2004 & 2006; Tawil, 2000). Critical adult education offers a strategy to locate, name and challenge violence embedded in the everyday lives of youth. This understanding can inform our grasp of everyday interpersonal conflicts such as bullying, by enhancing our understanding of how perceptions of the *enemy* or *otherness* develop (Pike & Selby, 2000; Reardon, 1988). By exploring violence within conflict, in combination with gaining insight into the forms of power that maintain violence, further insight into processes for community engagement, youth engagement, social action, and peace work can be discovered. Creating critical educational frameworks that encourage relationality, critical thinking, and dialogue; in combination with power analyses, can provide an opportunity to move one step closer to a society where a common value of respect for human dignity is manifested.

The impact of globalization, including the increased depictions of violations of human rights as observed in popular culture, requires adult educators (including young adult educators) to develop new strategies and ways of knowing to empower a culture for violence transformation and peace. Additionally, reduced federal funding for peace work (for example the closure of the Pearson Centre), has resulted in shrinking spaces for peace dialogue and the development of peaceful practices, and thus, adult educators have a critical role to play in creating pedagogical processes and learning spaces for peace.

Critical education within post-structural analyses are essential to understanding, deconstructing and reconstructing social relations where respect, plurality, and interconnections are centered. Furthermore, youth engagement in research and teaching in the area of violence transformation and peace work are essential towards building cultures of peace. Violence transformation needs a comprehensive and transdisciplinary approach (Pearce, 2011) that incorporates violence prevention (IHL), a social justice culture or positive peace (critical adult education), and intervention (peacebuilding skills and actions) (Bickmore, 2011). Complex issues, such as violence require space for creativity and the formation of alternative solutions. Thus, adult education requires a revolution in our educational frameworks as our existing frames cannot provide solutions to these contemporary, complex social realities. In this regard, Francis (2010) argues,

> Urgent is the work that needs to be done to develop theory on how we can demilitarize minds, societies and global systems in order to avoid the endless re-creation of violent histories, and to open up a very different kind of future for humanity. (p. 52)

Engaging young adults in peace work may create opportunities for new theoretical concepts of peace to emerge.

2 Opportunities and Recommendations: Future Research and Practice

Research, teaching, and learning for peace, often lacks a theoretical basis. Delving deep into the theoretical framework of peace work is essential to expose embedded assumptions, and to consider alternative pathways toward cultures of peace. Theoretical research is lacking in the area of peace work within critical adult education, and more work needs to be completed to explore the complexities of peace, violence and learning. A relational epistemology that examines how power is conceived and evaluated (referential dimension), how the study of violence is organized (structural dimension) and how engaged pedagogy is nurtured, offers a new framework within critical adult education to empower learning for peace. Additionally, a relational epistemology that de-centers the mind to embrace diverse ways of knowing and being (for example, as evident in Indigenous epistemologies) is a necessary next step in peacebuilding.

Secondly, the voices of youth are missing within adult education generally, and specifically within peace focused adult education. The risks associated with failing to engage youth in complex social issues such as violence, include adult education theory and practice, which lacks perspectives from a large, heterogeneous, and growing population within Canadian communities. The risks also include the creation of adult education strategies which fail to consider the forms of power interpenetrating within the lives of youth. Too often adults are creating peace pedagogies *for* youth and not *with* youth. The voices and perspectives of youth greatly enhance our understanding of violence and opportunities for building peace. More research with youth not already engaged in peace work would add to the perspectives shared. Additionally, more research with diverse youth (i.e. racial, gender, class, urban/rural), would add to the plurality of insights and experiences, thus contributing to a more holistic picture of violence and peace. Youth-centered research matters within adult education.

In addition to youth-centered research, youth engagement in peacebuilding education is essential. Adult educators can help identify and create points of entry for youth engagement in peace work, particularly within non-formal education. Adult educators have historically engaged people and communities to improve their lives through education and social action. Support, training, and collaboration in social action planning, particularly within youth-adult partnerships, would be an invaluable contribution to peacebuilding. Youth-adult partnerships and collaborations are being negatively impacted by the diminishing spaces for peace work and the decreasing spaces for intergenerational learning, such as reduced participation in faith based organizations. Adult educators need to reconsider the 'adult-only' focus in research, teaching and practice due to the positive outcomes stemming from youth-adult partnerships, including the collaborative possibilities within intergenerational learning.

Finally, given the influence of popular culture today, particularly within youth cultures, merging critical adult education with cultural studies is an integral piece to the overall picture of violence transformation and peacebuilding. More research is needed to specifically explore the role of popular culture in normalizing violence as well as the possibilities within popular culture to transform violence. By including popular culture within a critical adult education framework, new pedagogical tools may be fostered to challenge constructions of enmity and to challenge violence itself.

3   Conclusion

Critical adult education, centered on issues of power, ideology critique, relationality, voice, and participation, offers a means to expose how power maintains and enables the normalizations of violence, in order to challenge the *culture of violence*. Brand-Jacobsen (2002) argues the way to develop a "praxis for peace" is by "promoting a plurality of visions, alternatives and voices, and by building peace work on the search for creative and viable alternatives to violence, drawing on the background and experiences of actors at every social level" (p. 78). By engaging youth in social research on issues such as violence transformation, new insights into the lived experiences of youth can be revealed, valued, and incorporated in strategies for change. After all, "violence is preventable" (WHO, 2014, p. viii).

This study sought to explore how enmity constructions develop, how power influences these constructions, and how peace pedagogies can be realized towards enhancing peaceful practices. The dual analysis (ideology critique and pedagogical practice) was framed within a critical, collaborative, and PAR-inspired methodology, a methodology that enabled a rich, shared, and safe(r) learning space to critique violence and build peaceful communities. The participatory processes employed were central to this research.

The youth argue that enmity is constructed by learning that difference equals deficiency, through systems of exclusion, by enabling normalizations of violence to continue unquestioned, through disengaged citizenship or lack of relations, and through cultures of competition and rivalry. The youth also argue that by focusing on empowering individuals to engage in respectful and equitable relations, possibilities for peace exist. Beyond the analysis conducted by the youth, I argue that by merging harm reduction and values-based approaches (IHL – constructive peace), aspirations for social justice cultures (critical adult education – critical peace), and the centering of respectful relations and peaceful practices (peacebuilding education – empirical peace), within a relational epistemology, we advance one step closer to conditions where cultures of peace can exist and where respect for humanity is paramount. While I struggle with the complexity and significant consequences of violence, I am inspired by the resiliency and abilities of youth to create change, and hope that together we can find many pathways towards peace. In closing,

> The present culture of violence based on distrust, suspicion, intolerance and hatred, on the inability to interact constructively with all those who are different, must be replaced by a new culture based on non-violence, tolerance, mutual understanding and solidarity, on the ability to solve peacefully disputes and conflicts. (Symonides & Singh, 1996, p. 10)

Together, we can transform the present *culture of violence* toward building cultures of peace.

Note

1 In response to the prevention of a planned act of violence by three young adults in Halifax on February 14, 2015, Peter McKay referred to the accused as "murderous misfits."

APPENDIX 1

Guidelines for Photography

Title of Project: Creating Learning Spaces to Challenge & Transform Constructions of Enmity: Using Participatory Action Inspired Collaborative Research with Canadian Youth

1. Always ask permission before taking people's photos.
    Any photos with images of people require written consent (agreement) from the individuals in the photos. If the person is under age of 18, a parent or guardian must provide written consent. If certain people do not want their photo taken, respect their decision. A consent form is below.
2. When taking photos be safe.
    Be aware of what is around you (e.g. moving cars) and always stand on a solid surface.
3. Be prepared to explain what you are doing.
4. Respect the lives and safety of others.
    When you take photos for this project, think of people's safety first, and be respectful.

_____

Photo Consent Form

I am part of a research project. We are taking photographs talking about them with other people in small groups. Please sign this form if you agree to let me take your or your child's photograph for this project. You may decline and do not need to tell me why.

1. I agree to have my (or my child's) photo taken for this project:

Name: _____

Signature: _____

Date: _____

Please sign this form if you agree to let me use your photo in public such as a community photo show or an article in a journal. You may decline and do not need to tell me why.

2. I agree to my photo being used in public:

Name: _____

Signature: _____

Date: _____

Name of photographer: _____

* If you would like a copy of your picture, please write down your mailing address or email so I can send it to you:

_____

Adapted from: Lorenz, L & Webster, B. (n.d.) *Doing Your Own PhotoVoice Project: A Guide*. Retrieved Feb 15, 2013 from: *www.brainline.org*

APPENDIX 2

Guidelines for Informal Conversations & Interviews with Young Adults

- Open conversation reminding participant to please share information that they are comfortable sharing.
- Inquire if the location and context for the discussion is suitable/comfortable for the participant.
- Invite the participant to share their understandings of power and enmity as well as the use of photography to reflect upon constructions of enmity and power influences.
- Conclude with an invitation for the participant to develop questions for the focus group and to select a photo(s) to share with group for further discussions and learning (if comfortable).

APPENDIX 3

Community Standards

* The *rules* below were generated by the participants to help create a safer space for our critical work.

Conflict can be an opportunity

Don't have to speak

Respect

Hear Everyone Out

Respect different learning styles

Not speaking over each other

Be open & open-minded

Agree to disagree

Using inclusive language [Don't say anything inappropriate]

Positive in what we say about other people

We all have knowledge

All knowledge is partial

Not one answer

Glossary

Conflict an inevitable social process of disagreement, which can lead to social change.

Cultural violence The attitudinal and belief processes that encourage direct and structural violence to manifest without question (for example religion or language) (Galtung, 1996).

Culture of peace A culture of peace is "more than an absence of war...it means justice and equity for all as the basis for living together in harmony and free from violence" (UNESCO, 2002, p. 1).

Direct violence A behaviour or an incident where violence is physically or verbally enacted, "harming the body, mind or spirit" (Galtung, 1996, p. 31).

Enemy A term to describe the *other* as inferior or someone/group whose human dignity is not valued. The Latin origins of the term infer 'not' 'friend', and is defined by hostility, harm or injury toward another ("Enemy," 1995).

Negative peace "The absence of violence of all kinds" (Galtung, 1996, p. 31).

Peace work Approaches and practices aimed at reducing and preventing violence through non-violence and peaceful processes.

Peacebuilding education The practices and processes aimed toward building or rebuilding healthy relations.

Positive peace The presence of social justice and equity achieved through cooperation, dialogue, integration, and solidarity (Galtung, 1996).

Power A complex, contentious, and relational concept that exists in multiple forms and spaces (Gaventa, 2006). Power is "the ability to create something, to make something happen or to influence or change something or someone" (Francis, 2010, p. 114).

Structural violence Inequitable processes located within social structures, such as racism and sexism (Galtung, 1996).

Violence A social phenomenon which includes "the intentional use of physical force or power, threatened or actual, against oneself, another person, or against a group or community, that either results in or has a high likelihood of resulting in injury, death, psychological harm, maldevelopment, or deprivation" (WHO, 2002, p. 5).

Young adult Persons between the ages of 18–29 (UN, 2011).

Youth Persons between the ages of 15–24 (UNESCO, 2011).

References

Aberton, H. (2011). Challenging constructed learner identities: Women's informal learning. In S. Jackson (Ed.), *Lifelong learning and social justice: Communities, work and identities in a globalised world*. Leicester: NIACE.

Agger, B. (1991). Critical theory, poststructuralism, postmodernism: Their sociological relevance. *Annual Review of Sociology, 17*, 105–131.

Anderson, A. (n.d.). *The community builders approach to theory of change: A practical guide to theory development*. New York, NY: The Aspen Institute.

Andreotti, V. (2011). *Actionable postcolonial theory in education*. Basingstoke: Palgrave Macmillan.

Apple, M. (2005). Making critical pedagogy strategic – on doing critical educational work in conservative times. In I. Gur-Ze'ev (Ed.), *Critical theory and critical pedagogy today: Toward a new critical language in education*. Israel: University of Haifa.

Apple, M. (2011). Global crises, social justice, and teacher education. *Journal of Teacher Education, 62*(2), 222–234.

Auld, A., & Tutton, M. (2015, February 14). McKay says Halifax plot would have been 'devastating,' but no terror link. *Metro News*. Retrieved from http://metronews.ca/news/halifax/1288145/mackay-says-halifax-plot-would-have-been-devastating-but-no-terror-link/

Barker, C. (2004). *The sage dictionary of cultural studies*. London, Thousand Oaks, CA, & New Delhi: Sage Publications.

Barker, C. (2008). *Cultural studies: Theory and practice*. London: Sage Publications.

Berger, P., & Luckmann, T. (1966). *The social construction of reality: A treatise in the sociology of knowledge*. Garden City, NY: Doubleday.

Bergum, V. (2003). Relational pedagogy. Embodiment, improvisation, and interdependence. *Nursing Philosophy, 4*(2), 121–128.

Bhabha, H. (1990). *Nation and narration*. New York, NY: Routledge.

Bickmore, K. (2004). Discipline or democracy? School districts management of conflict and social exclusion. *Theory and Research in Social Education, 32*(1), 75–97.

Bickmore, K. (2006). Democratic social cohesion (assimilation?) representations of social conflict in Canadian public school curriculum. *Canadian Journal of Education, 29*(2), 359–386.

Bickmore, K. (2011). Policies and programming for safer schools: Are anti-bullying approaches impeding education for peacebuilding? *Educational Policy, 25*(4), 648–687.

Bohan, C., Doppen, F., Feinberg, J., & O'Mahoney, C. (2008). Citizens of today and tomorrow: An exploration of preservice social studies teachers' knowledge and their professors' experience with citizenship. *Curriculum & Teaching Dialogue, 10*(1), 117–134.

Boulding, E. (1996). *Peace behaviors in various societies. In: From a culture of violence to a culture of peace*. Paris: UNESCO Publishing.

Brand-Jacobsen, K. (2002). Peace: The goal and the way. In J. Galtung, G. Jacobsen, & K. Brand-Jacobsen (Eds.), *Searching for peace: The road to transcend*. London: Pluto Press.

Breire, J., & Jordan, C. E. (2004). Violence against women: Outcome complexity and implications for assessment and treatment. *Journal of Interpersonal Violence, 19*(11), 1252–1276.

Briton, D. (1996). *Modern practice of adult education: A postmodern critique*. Albany, NY: State University of New York Press.

Brookfield, S. (2005). *The power of critical theory: Learning adult learning and teaching*. San Francisco, CA: Jossey-Bass.

Brookfield, S. (2009). The concept of critical reflection: Promises and contradictions. *European Journal of Social Work, 12*(3), 293–304.

Brown, L. D. (2002). People-centered development and participatory research. In R. Tandon (Ed.), *Participatory research: Revisiting the roots*. New Delhi: Mosaic Books.

Brownlee, J., & Berthelsen, D. (2008). Developing relational epistemology through relational pedagogy: New ways of thinking about personal epistemology in teacher education. In M. Swe Khine (Ed.), *Knowin, knowledge and beliefs: Epistemological studies across diverse disciplines*. New York, NY: Springer.

Bryceson, D., Manicom, L., & Kassam, Y. (2002). The methodology of the participatory research approach. In R. Tandon (Ed.), *Participatory research: Revisiting the roots*. New Delhi: Mosaic Books.

Bush, K., & Saltarelli, D. (2000). *The two faces of education in ethnic conflict: Towards a peacebuilding education for children*. Florence, Italy: UNICEF.

Butler, J. (2010). *Frames of war: When is life greivable?* London: Verso.

Cairns, J., & Sears, A. (2012). *The democratic imagination: Envisioning popular power in the twenty-first century*. Toronto: University of Toronto Press.

Canadian Broadcasting Company (CBC). (2014a, December 5). Retrieved from http://www.cbc.ca/news/canada/dutch-man-suspected-of-tormenting-amanda-todd-had-75-other-victims-facebook-report-says-1.2857281

Canadian Broadcasting Company (CBC). (2014b, November 29). Retrieved from http://www.cbc.ca/news/canada/nova-scotia/rehtaeh-parsons-society-to-launch-saturday-1.2854158

Canadian Broadcasting Company (CBC). (2015a, January 15). Retrieved from http://www.cbc.ca/news/canada/nova-scotia/rehtaeh-parsons-case-teen-in-explicit-photo-gets-probation-1.2901502

Canadian Broadcasting Company (CBC). (2015b, January 25). Retrieved from http://www.cbc.ca/news/canada/nova-scotia/raymond-taavel-memorial-discussed-in-halifax-1.2737279

Canadian Broadcasting Company (CBC). (2017, March 16). Retrieved from http://www.cbc.ca/news/world/aydin-coban-sentenced-netherlands-online-fraud-blackmail-1.4027359

Canadian Council for International Cooperation (CCIC). (2008). *Focus on ethics: Addressing tensions in choosing fundraising images*. Ottawa: CCIC.

Canadian Encyclopedia. (2015, January 25). Retrieved from http://www.thecanadianencyclopedia.ca/en/article/edward-cornwallis/

Canadian Institutes of Health Research, Natural Sciences and Engineering Research Council of Canada, and Social Sciences and Humanities Research Council of Canada. (2010, December). *Tri-council policy statement: Ethical conduct for research involving humans*. Ottawa: Government of Canada.

Canadian Red Cross. (2013, May 16). *Even wars have limits*. Retrieved from http://www.redcross.ca/article.asp?id=27425&tid=062

Carr, P., & Thesee, G. (2012). Discursive epistemologies by, for and about the decolonizing project. In A. Abdi (Ed.), *Decolonizing philosophies of education*. Boston, MA: Sense Publishers.

Carter, C. (2010). Teacher preparation for peace education. In C. Carter (Ed.), *Conflict resolution and peace education: transformations across disciplines*. New York, NY: Palgrave Macmillan.

Chase, S. (2015, March 10). Niqabs 'rooted in a culture that is anti-women,' Harper says. *The Global and Mail*. Retrieved from http://www.theglobeandmail.com/news/politics/niqabs-rooted-in-a-culture-that-is-anti-women-harper-says/article23395242/

Children and Youth in Challenging Contexts Network. (2014a). *Youth engagement: Empowering youth voices to improve services, programs, and policy*. Halifax, NS: Children and Youth in Challenging Contexts Network.

Children and Youth in Challenging Contexts Network. (2014b). *Coping with violence: Promising practices for child and youth mental health*. Halifax, NS: Children and Youth in Challenging Contexts Network.

Chilisa, B. (2012). *Indigenous research methodologies*. Los Angeles, CA: Sage Publications.

Chovanec, D., & Lange, E. (2007). Learning in community. In L. Savage & T. Fenwick (Eds.), *Learning in community: Proceedings of the joint international conference of the Adult Education Research Conference (AERC) (48th National Conference) and the Canadian Association for the Study of Adult Education (CASAE)/l'Association Cannadienne our l'Etude des Adultes (ACEEA) (26th National Conference)*. Halifax, NS: Canadian Association for the Study of Adult Education.

Christens, B., & Dolan, T. (2011). Interweaving youth development, community development, and social change through youth organizing. *Youth & Society, 43*(2), 528–548.

Collin Marks, S., & Marks, J. (2002). What do they want me to do? In J. P. Lederach & J. Moomaw Jenner (Eds.), *A handbook of international peacebuilding: Into the eye of the storm*. San Francisco, CA: Jossey-Bass.

REFERENCES

Conti, J., & O'Neil, M. (2007). Studying power: Qualitative methods and the global elite. *Qualitative Research, 7*(1), 63–82.

Creswell, J. (1994). *Research design: Qualitative and quantitative approaches.* New York, NY: Sage Publications.

Creswell, J. (2007). *Educational research: Planning, conducting, and evaluating quantitative and qualitative research* (3rd ed.). Columbus, OH: Pearson.

Dalhousie University. (2015, January 5). Retrieved from http://www.dal.ca/news/media/media-release/2015/01/05/dalhousie_suspends_13_-fourth_year_dental_students_from_clinical_activities_.html

Davies, B. (2010). What do we mean by youth work? In J. Batsleer & B. Davies (Eds.), *What is youth work? Empowering youth and community work practice.* Exeter: Learning Matters Ltd.

DeKrai, M., Bulling, D., McLean, C., & Fletcher, B. (2010). Youth encouraging support: A unique youth education/advocacy initiative to reduce the stigma of mental illness. In W. Linds, L. Goulet, & A. Sammel (Eds.), *Emancipatory practices: Adult/youth engagement for social and environmental justice.* Rotterdam, The Netherlands: Sense Publishers.

Ellsworth, E. (1992). Why doesn't this feel empowering: Working through the repressive myths of critical pedagogy. In C. Luke & J. Gore (Eds.), *Feminisms and critical pedagogy.* New York, NY: Routledge.

Enemy. (1995). *The concise Oxford dictionary of current English* (9th ed.). Oxford: Claredon Press.

English, L., & Mayo, P. (2012). *Learning with adults: A critical pedagogical introduction.* Boston, MA: Sense Publishers.

Fals-Borda, O., & Rahman, M. (1991). *Action and knowledge: Breaking the monopoly with participatory action-research.* New York, NY: The Apex Press.

Foucault, M. (1979). The means of correct training. In *Discipline and punish: The birth of the prison* (pp. 170–194). New York, NY: Vintage.

Foucault, M. (1982). The subject and power. *Critical Inquiry, 8*(4), 777–794.

Foucault, M. (2000). *Power.* New York, NY: New York Press.

Francis, D. (2002). *People, peace and power: Conflict transformation in action.* New York, NY: Pluto Press.

Francis, D. (2010). *From pacification to peacebuilding: A call to global transformation.* New York, NY: Pluto Press.

Frantzi, K. (2004). Human rights education: The United Nations endeavour and the importance of childhood and intelligent sympathy. *International Education Journal, 5*(1), 1–8.

Freire, P. (1970). *Pedagogy of the oppressed.* New York, NY: Herder and Herder.

Freire, P. (1985). *The politics of education: Culture, power, and liberation.* South Hadley, MA: Bergin & Gaivery Publishers.

Freire, P. (2003). *Pedagogy of the oppressed.* New York, NY: Continuum.

Freire, P. (2004). *Pedagogy of indignation.* Boulder, CO: Paradigm Publishers.

Freire, P. (2005). *Teachers as cultural workers: Letters to those who dare to teach.* Boulder, CO: Westview Press.

Fresard, J.-J. (2004). *The roots of behavior in war.* Geneva: International Committee of the Red Cross.

Galtung, J. (1969). Violence, peace and peace research. *Journal of Peace Research, 6*(3), 167–191.

Galtung, J. (1983). Peace education: Learning to hate war, love peace, and to do something about it. *International Review of Education, 29*(3), 281–287.

Galtung, J. (1990). Cultural violence. *Journal of Peace Research, 27,* 291–305.

Galtung, J. (1996). *Peace by peaceful means: Peace and conflict, development and civilization.* Oslo: International Peace Research Institute.

Galtung, J., & Tschudi, F. (2002). Crafting peace: On the psychology of the TRANSEND approach. In J. Galtung, C. Jacobsen, & K. Brand-Jacobsen (Eds.), *Searching for peace: The road to transcend.* London: Pluto Press.

Gaventa, J. (1980). *Power and powerlessness: Quiescence and rebellion in an Appalachian Valley.* Chicago, IL: University of Illinois Press.

Gaventa, J. (2006). Finding space for change: A power analysis. *IDS Bulletin, 3*(6), 23–33.

Gaventa, J. (2007). Finding the spaces for change: A power analysis. In R. Eyben, J. Pettit, & C. Harris (Eds.), *Exploring power for change* (IDS Bulletin 37.6). Brighton: IDS. Retrieved from http://bulletin.ids.ac.uk/idsbo/article/view/898

Gaventa, J., & Cornwall, A. (2007). Power and knowledge. In P. Reason & H. Bradbury (Eds.), *The Sage handbook of action research* (2nd ed., pp. 172–189). Thousand Oaks, CA: Sage Publications.

Gaventa, J., & Merrifield, J. (2002). Participatory research in North America and India. In R. Tandon (Ed.), *Participatory research: Revisiting the roots.* New Delhi: Mosaic Books.

Giroux, H. (1993). *Living dangerously: Multiculturalism and the politics of difference.* New York, NY: Peter Lang.

Giroux, H. (1996). *Fugitive cultures: Race, violence and youth.* New York, NY & London: Routledge.

Giroux, H. (2011). Fighting for the future: American youth and the global struggle for democracy. *Cultural Studies – Critical Methodologies, 11*(4), 328–240.

Gore, J. (1992). What we can do for you! What can "we" do for "you"?: Struggling over empowerment in critical and feminist pedagogy. In C. Luke & J. Gore (Eds.), *Feminisms and critical pedagogy.* New York, NY: Routledge.

Government of Canada. (2014, October 14). Retrieved from http://news.gc.ca/web/article-en.do?mthd=tp&crtr.page=20&nid=892509&crtr.tp1D=1&_ga=1.96613599.1931468925.1413466642

Greenberg Research Inc. (1999). *The people on war report: ICRC worldwide consultation on the rules of war.* Geneva: ICRC.

Guba, E. G., & Lincoln, Y. S. (1994). Competing paradigms in qualitative research. In N. K. Denzin & Y. S. Lincoln (Eds.), *Handbook of qualitative research* (pp. 105–117). Thousand Oaks, CA: Sage Publications.

Guo, S. (2009). Difference, deficiency, and devaluation: Tracing the roots of non-recognition of foreign credentials for immigrant professionals in Canada. *The Canadian Journal for the Study of Adult Education, 22*(1), 37–52.

Hakvoort, I., & Oppenheimer, L. (1999). Understanding peace and war: A review of developmental psychology research. *Developmental Review, 18,* 353–389.

Hall, B. (2002). Breaking the monopoly of knowledge: Research methods, participation, and development. In R. Tandon (Ed.), *Participatory research: Revisiting the roots.* New Delhi: Mosaic Books.

Harris, C. (2008). Transformative education in violence contexts: Working with Muslim and Christian youth in Kaduna, Nigeria. *IDS Bulletin, 40*(3), 34–40.

Hayward, C. (2000). *De-facing power.* New York, NY: Cambridge University Press.

Hayward, C. (2006). On power and responsibility. *Political Studies Review, 4,* 156–163.

Hayward, C. (2013). *How Americans make race.* New York, NY: Cambridge University Press.

Hayward, C., & Lukes, S. (2008). Nobody to shoot? Power, structure, and agency: A dialogue. *Journal of Power, 1*(1), 5–20.

hooks, b. (2003). *Teaching community: A pedagogy of hope.* New York, NY: Routledge.

hooks, b. (2010). *Teaching critical thinking: Practical wisdom.* New York, NY: Routledge.

Howard Ross, M. (2000). Creating the conditions for peacemaking: Theories of practice in ethnic conflict resolution. *Ethnic and Racial Studies, 22*(6), 1002–1034.

Huber, L. (2009). Disrupting apartheid of knowledge: Testimonio as methodology in Latina/o critical race research in education. *International Journal of Qualitative Studies in Education, 22*(6), 639–654.

Hunjan, R., & Pettit, J. (2011). *Power: A practical guide for facilitating social change.* Dunfermline: Carnegie United Kingdom Trust.

Huq, R. (2002). Urban unrest in Northern England 2001: Rhetoric and reality behind the 'race riots.' In A. Lentin (Ed.), *Learning from violence: The youth dimension.* Budapest: Council of Europe Publishing.

International Committee of the Red Cross. (2004). *Training – education – awareness: ICRC annual report 2004.* Geneva: International Committee of the Red Cross.

International Committee of the Red Cross. (2006). *Exploring humanitarian law project summary.* Geneva: International Committee of the Red Cross.

International Committee of the Red Cross. (2011). *Children affected by armed conflict and other situations of violence.* Geneva: International Committee of Red Cross.

Jackson, S. (2011). Lifelong learning and social justice: Introduction. In S. Jackson (Ed.), *Lifelong learning and social justice: communities, work and identities in a globalised world*. Leicester: NIACE.

Jones, M., & Yonezawa, S. (2010). Adult and youth engagement in democratic inquiry for educational change. In W. Linds, L. Goulet, & A. Sammel (Eds.), *Emancipatory practices: Adult/youth engagement for social and environmental justice*. Rotterdam, The Netherlands: Sense Publishers.

Kaufman, J., & Williams, K. (2010). *Women and war gender identity and activism in times of conflict*. Sterling, VA: Kumarian Press.

Keashly, L., & Warters, W. (2000). Working it out: Conflict in interpersonal contexts. In L. Fisk & J. Schellenberg (Eds.), *Patterns of conflict: Paths to peace*. Peterborough: Broadview Press.

Kellner, D. (2005). Critical theory and education: Historical and metatheoretical perspectives. In I. Gur-Ze'ev (Ed.), *Critical theory and critical pedagogy today: Toward a new critical language in education*. Israel: University of Haifa.

Kincheloe, J. (2009). Critical complexity and participatory action research: Decolonizing "democratic" knowledge production. In D. Kapoor & S. Jordan (Eds.), *Education, participatory action research and social change: International perspectives*. New York, NY: Palgrave McMillan.

Kirby, K., Greaves, L., & Reid, C. (2010). *Experience research social change: Methods beyond mainstream*. Toronto: University of Toronto Press.

Lange, E. (2015). Transformative learning and concepts of the self: Insights from immigrant and intercultural journeys. *International Journal of Lifelong Education, 34*(6), 623–642.

Lange, E., & Chubb, A. (2009). Critical environment adult education in Canada: Student environmental activism. *New Directions for Adult and Continuing Education, 214*, 61–72.

Lather, P. (1992). Critical frames in educational research: Feminist and post-structural perspectives. *Theory into Practice, 31*(2), 87–99.

Lear, J. (2006). *Radical hope: Ethics in the face of cultural devastation*. Cambridge, MA & London: Harvard University Press.

Lederach, J. P. (2006). Defining conflict transformation. *Peacework, 33*, 26–27.

Lee, E. (2012). Escape, retreat, revolt: Queer people of color living in Montreal using photovoice as a tool for community organizing. In A. Choudrey, J. Hanley, & E. Shragge (Eds.), *Building from the local for global justice*. Oakland, CA: PM Press.

Lewis, M. (1992). Interrupting patriarchy: Politics, resistance and transformation in the feminist classroom. In C. Luke & J. Gore (Eds.), *Feminisms and critical pedagogy*. New York, NY: Routledge.

Linds, W., & Goulet, L. (2010). (Un) intentional spaces. In W. Linds, L. Goulet, & A. Sammel (Eds.), *Emancipatory practices: Adult/youth engagement for social and environmental justice*. Rotterdam, The Netherlands: Sense Publishers.

Luke, C., & Gore, J. (1992). *Feminisms and critical pedagogy*. New York, NY: Routledge.

REFERENCES

Lukes, S. (1974). *Power: A radical view*. Basingstoke: Macmillan.

Lukes, S. (2005). *Power: A radical view*. Basingstoke: Macmillan.

Manzo, L. C., & Brightgill, N. (2007). Towards a participatory ethics. In S. Kindon, R. Pain, & M. Kesby (Eds.), *Participatory action research approaches and methods: Connecting people, participation and place*. New York, NY: Routledge.

Mayo, P. (1999). *Gramsci, Freire and adult education: Possibilities for transformative action*. New York, NY: Palgrave MacMillan.

McEvoy-Levy, S. (2001). Youth, violence, and conflict transformation. *Peace Review, 13*(1), 89–96.

McGregor, C. (2010). Irreconcilable differences?: Youth-adult partnerships in a civic and legal literacy research project. In W. Linds, L. Goulet, & A. Sammel (Eds.), *Emancipatory practices: Adult/youth engagement for social and environmental justice*. Rotterdam, The Netherlands: Sense Publishers.

McLaren, P. (2005). Critical pedagogy in the age of terror. In I. Gur-Ze'ev (Ed.), *Critical theory and critical pedagogy today: Toward a new critical language in education*. Israel: University of Haifa.

Merriam, S. (2009). *Qualitative research: A guide to design and implementation*. San Francisco, CA: Jossey-Bass.

Merriam, S. (2010). Globalization and the role of adult and continuing education: Challenges and opportunities. In C. Kasworm, A. Rose, and J. Ross-Gordon (Eds.), *Handbook of adult and continuing education*. Los Angeles, CA: Sage Publications.

Mertens, D. (2009). *Transformative research and evaluation*. New York, NY: The Guilford Press.

Mohanty, C. (2003). *Feminism without borders: Decolonizing theory, practicing solidarity*. Durham, NC: Duke University Press.

Morrow, R. (1994). *Critical theory and methodology*. Thousand Oaks, CA: Sage Publications.

Mullaly, B. (2010). *Challenging oppression and confronting privilege: A critical social work approach*. Toronto: Oxford University Press.

Nabavi, M., & Lund, D. (2010). Youth and social justice: A conversation on collaborative activism. In W. Linds, L. Goulet, & A. Sammel (Eds.), *Emancipatory practices: Adult/youth engagement for social and environmental justice*. Rotterdam, The Netherlands: Sense Publishers.

Nesbit, T. (2013). Canadian adult education: A critical tradition. In T. Nesbit, S. Brigham, N. Taber, & T. Fenwick (Eds.), *Building on critical traditions: Adult education and learning in Canada*. Toronto: Thompson Education Publishing.

Ng, R. (1995). Teaching against the grain. In R. Ng, P. A. Staton, & J. Scare (Eds.), *Anti-racism, feminism, and approaches to education*. Westport, CT: Greenwood Publishing.

Orner, M. (1992). Interrupting the calls for student voice in "liberatory" education: A feminist post-structural perspective. In C. Luke & J. Gore (Eds.), *Feminisms and critical pedagogy*. New York, NY: Routledge.

Orsini, A. (2010). Learning without teaching: Youth-led programs to reduce car trips to school. In W. Linds, L. Goulet, & A. Sammel (Eds.), *Emancipatory practices: Adult/youth engagement for social and environmental justice*. Rotterdam, The Netherlands: Sense Publishers.

Pain, R., Kesby, M., & Kindon, S. (2007). Conclusion: The space(s) and scale(s) of participatory action research: Constructing empowering geographies? In S. Kindon, R. Pain, & M. Kesby (Eds.), *Participatory action research approaches and methods: Connecting people, participation and place*. New York, NY: Routledge.

Parker, C. (2012). *Inclusion in peacebuilding education: Discussion of diversity and conflict as learning opportunities for migrant students* (Unpublished doctoral dissertation). Toronto: Ontario Institute for Studies in Education.

Pantazidou, M. (2012). *What next for power analysis? A review of recent experiences with the power cube and related frameworks*. Sussex: IDS Working Paper.

Peaceful Schools International. (2015). *Peaceful schools international*. Retrieved from http://peacefulschoolsinternational.org/about

Pearce, J. (2007). *Violence, power and participation: Building citizenship in contexts of chronic violence*. Brighton: University of Sussex Institute of Development Studies.

Pearce, J. (2009). Introduction: Research democracy and social change with violence in the foreground. *IDS Bulletin, 40*(3), 1–9.

Pearce, J. (2013, July 12). *Bringing violence into the power cube*. Retrieved from http://www.powercube.net/wp-content/uploads/2009/11/violence_powercube.pdf

Pike, G., & Selby, D. (2000). *In the global classroom 1*. Toronto: Pippin Publishing.

Podd, W. (2011). Participation. In J. Batsleer & B. Davies (Eds.), *What is youth work? Empowering youth and community work practice*. Exeter: Learning Matters Ltd.

PREVNet. (2015, May 19). *Cyberbullying*. Retrieved from http://www.prevnet.ca/research/bullying-statistics/cyberbullying

Price, L. S. (2005). *Feminist framework: Building theory on violence against women*. Nova Scotia: Fernwood.

Quinn Patton, M. (2002). *Qualitative research and evaluation methods* (3rd ed.). Thousand Oaks, CA: Sage Publications.

Ramberg, I. (2003). *Learning from violence: Youth policy responses to everyday violence symposium report*. Budapest: Council of Europe Publishing.

Raviv, A., Oppenheimer, L., & Bar-Tal, D. (1999). Why study children's and adolescents' understanding of peace, conflict, and war? In A. Raviv, L. Oppenheimer, & D. Bar-Tal (Eds.), *How children understand war and peace: A call for international peace education*. San Francisco, CA: Jossey-Bass Publishers.

Reardon, B. (1988). *Comprehensive peace education: Educating for global responsibility*. New York, NY: Teachers College Press.

Reardon, B. (1993). *Women and peace: Feminist visions of global security*. New York, NY: State University of New York Press.

Rezow-Rashi, G. (1995). Multicultural education, anti-racist education, and critical pedagogy: Reflections on everyday practices. In R. Ng, P. Staton, & J. Scane (Eds.), *Anti-racism, feminism, and critical approaches to education*. Westport, CT, & London: Bergin & Garvey.

Riordon, M. (2011). *Our way to fight: Peace-work under siege in Israel-Palestine*. Toronto: Pluto Press.

Ross, L., Downs, T., Tejani, A., Dezan, R., & Lowe, K. (2010). Trust, preparation, transparency, and reflection: Negotiating roles in youth-adult partnerships for social and environmental justice. In W. Linds, L. Goulet, & A. Sammel (Eds.), *Emancipatory practices: Adult/youth engagement for social and environmental justice*. Rotterdam, The Netherlands: Sense Publishers.

Said, E. (1978). *Orientalism*. New York, NY: Random House.

Said, E. (2000). Invention, memory, and place. *Critical Inquiry, 26*(2), 175–192.

Sawchuck, P. (2010). Action and power: Everyday life and development of working class groups. In P. Sawchuck, N. Duarte, & M. Elhammoumi (Eds.), *Critical perspectives on activity: Explorations across education, work, and everyday life*. New York, NY: Cambridge University Press.

Schirch, L. (2013). *Conflict assessment and peacebuilding planning: Toward a participatory approach to human security*. Boulder, CO: Kumarian Press.

Shor, I. (1992). *Empowering education: Critical teaching for social change*. Chicago, IL: University of Chicago Press.

Shultz, L. (2012). Decolonizing social justice education: from policy knowledge to citizenship action. In A. Abdi (Ed.), *Decolonizing philosophies of education*. Boston, MA: Sense Publishers.

Sidorkin, A. (2002). *Learning relations: Impure education, de-schooled schools, and dialogue with evil*. New York, NY: Peter Lang.

Smith, L. T. (1999). Research through imperial eyes. In L. T. Smith (Ed.), *Decolonizing methodologies: Research and indigenous peoples* (pp. 42–57). London & New York, NY: Zed Books.

Spivak, G. C. (1990). *The post-colonial critic: Interviews, strategies, dialogues*. New York, NY & London: Routledge.

Statistics Canada. (2013). *What has changed for young people in Canada*. Ottawa: Government of Canada.

Statistics Canada. (2013a, February 5). *2011 census*. Ottawa: Government of Canada.

Statistics Canada. (2013b, May 28). *Children and youth*. Retrieved from http://www5.statcan.gc.ca/subject-sujet/result-resultat.action?pid=20000&id=-20000&lang=eng&type=SDDS&pageNum=1&more=0

Stephenson, M., & Zanotti, L. (2012). *Peacebuilding through community-based NGO's: Paradoxes and possibilities*. Sterling, VA: Kumarian Press.

Stuttaford, M., & Coe, C. (2007). Participatory learning: Opportunities and challenges. In S. Kindon, R. Pain, & M. Kesby (Eds.), *Participatory action research approaches and methods: Connecting people, participation and place*. New York, NY: Routledge.

Susskind, Y. (2010). An empowerment framework for understanding, planning, and evaluating youth-adult engagement in community activism. In W. Linds, L. Goulet, & A. Sammel (Eds.), *Emancipatory practices: Adult/youth engagement for social and environmental justice*. Rotterdam, The Netherlands: Sense Publishers.

Symonides, J., & Singh, K. (1996). Constructing a culture of peace: Challenges and perspectives – an introductory note. In *From a culture of violence to a culture of peace*. Paris: UNESCO Publishing.

Tandon, R. (2002a). Social transformation and participatory research. In R. Tandon (Ed.), *Participatory research: Revisiting the roots*. New Delhi: Mosaic Books.

Tandon, R. (2002b). Participatory research, educational experience and empowerment of adults. In R. Tandon (Ed.), *Participatory research: Revisiting the roots*. New Delhi: Mosaic Books.

Tandon, R. (2002c). Knowledge as power. In R. Tandon (Ed.). Participatory research: Revisiting the roots. New Delhi: Mosaic Books.

Tandon, R. (2002d). Knowledge, participation and empowerment: PRIA's experience. In R. Tandon (Ed.), *Participatory research: Revisiting the roots*. New Delhi: Mosaic Books.

Tawil, S. (2000). International humanitarian law and basic education. *International Review of the Red Cross, 839*, 581–599.

Tcherepashenets, N. (2011). Transformations: Lifelong learners in the era of globalisation. In S. Jackson (Ed.), *Lifelong learning and social justice: communities, work and identities in a globalised world*. Leicester: NIACE.

Thayer-Bacon, B. (1999). How can caring help? A personalized cross-generational examination of violent adolescent experiences in school. In L. Rennie Forcey & I. Murray-Harris (Eds.), *Peacebuilding for adolescents: Strategies for educators and community leaders*. New York, NY: Peter Lang.

Thayer-Bacon, B. (2003). *Relational "(e)pistemologies."* New York, NY: Peter Lang.

Thayer-Bacon, B. (2010). A pragmatist and feminist relational (e)pistemology. *European Journal of Pragmatism and American Philosophy, 2*(1), 1–22.

Tisdell, E. (1993). Feminism and adult learning: Power, pedagogy, and praxis. In S. B. Merriam (Ed.), *New directions for adult and continuing education* (pp. 91–103). San Francisco, CA: Jossey-Bass Publishers.

Toh, S.-H. (2002). Peace building and peace education: Local experiences, global reflections. *Prospects, 32*(1), 87–93.

United Nations. (1998). *UN 1998 resolution 52 session agenda item 156 A/RES/52/1315 January 1998 culture of peace*. New York, NY: United Nations.

United Nations Department of Economic and Social Affairs. (2011). *International migration in a globalizing world: The role of youth*. New York, NY: UNDESA.

United Nations Education, Scientific, and Cultural Organization. (1986). *The Seville Statement on violence.* Paris: UNESCO.

United Nations Education, Scientific, and Cultural Organization. (1995). *Strategy on human rights 1996–2001.* Paris: UNESCO.

United Nations Educational, Scientific, and Cultural Organization (UNESCO). (2002). *Mainstreaming the culture of peace.* Paris: UNESCO.

United Nations Educational, Scientific, and Cultural Organization (UNESCO). (2004). *Empowering youth through national policies.* Paris: UNESCO.

United Nations Education, Scientific, and Cultural Organization (UNESCO). (2011). *United Nations world youth report 2010.* Paris: UNESCO.

United Nations Population Fund (UNFPA). (2011). *State of the world population in 2011: People and possibilities in a world of 7 billion.* New York, NY: UNFPA.

Veneklasen, L., & Miller, V. (2002). *A new weave of power, people, and politics: The action guide for advocacy and citizen participation.* Warwickshire: Practical Action Publishing.

Walby, S. (2009). *Globalization and inequities: Complexity and contested modernities.* Los Angeles, CA & London: Sage Publications.

Warner, A., Langlois, M., & Dumand, C. (2010). Voices from youth action teams: Creating successful partnerships for community action. In W. Linds, L. Goulet, & A.Sammel (Eds.), *Emancipatory practices: Adult/youth engagement for social and environmental justice.* Rotterdam, The Netherlands: Sense Publishers.

Weil, M. (2013). *The handbook of community practice.* London: Sage Publications.

Wilson, S. (2008). *Research is ceremony: Indigenous research methods.* Black Point, NS: Fernwood Publishing.

Winfield, B. (1999). Community-based service: Re-creating the beloved community. In L. Rennie Forcey & I. Murray-Harris (Eds.), *Peacebuilding for adolescents: Strategies for educators and community leaders.* New York, NY: Peter Lang.

Wink, J. (2011). *Critical pedagogy: Notes from the real world.* Toronto: Pearson.

Wlodkowski, R. (2008). *Enhancing adult motivation to learn: A comprehensive guide to teaching all adults.* San Francisco, CA: Jossey-Bass.

World Health Organization. (2002). *World report on violence and health.* Geneva: World Health Organization.

World Health Organization. (2014). *Global status report on violence prevention 2014.* Geneva: World Health Organization.

World Health Organization. (2016). *Global plan of action to prevent violence.* Geneva: World Health Organization.

Wright, H. (2000). Why write back to the new missionaries? Addressing the exclusion of (Black) others from discourses of empowerment. In G. Dei & A. Calliste (Eds.), *Power, knowledge and anti-racism education.* Halifax, NS: Fernwood Publishing.

Zelizer, C., & Rubinstein, R. (2009). Creating structure and capacity for peace. In C. Zeilzer & R. Rubinstein (Eds.), *Building peace: Practical reflections from the field*. Sterling, VA: Kumarian Press.

Zingaro, L. (2009). *Speaking out: Storytelling for social change*. Walnut Creek, CA: Left Coast Press.

Zizek, S. (2008). *Violence*. New York, NY: Picador.

Index

Collaborative learning   22, 31, 32, 36, 42, 60–63, 92, 103, 107, 111, 112, 116, 119
Competition (& Rivalry)   45, 54–56, 60, 63, 71, 85, 90, 116, 120
Conflict   1, 2, 4, 5, 8, 10, 11, 18, 20, 22–29, 31, 32, 34, 35, 40, 44, 45, 48, 49, 54–56, 58–63, 66, 71–74, 77, 81, 83, 85, 86, 93, 95–103, 106, 108, 109, 113, 115–117, 121, 123, 128
Conflict transformation   1, 2, 20, 22, 24, 26–28, 32, 34, 44, 59, 72, 74, 85, 86, 98, 106
Critical adult education   20, 21, 26, 27, 44, 45, 65, 87, 91, 94–103, 106, 109, 111, 113, 114, 116–120
Critical pedagogy   21, 22, 25, 26, 39, 40, 45, 53, 56, 59, 87, 96, 98, 106, 114, 116
Cultural violence   7, 50–52, 57–59, 94, 116
Culture of peace   7, 8, 18, 27, 29, 31, 77–81, 85, 103

Difference (Deficient)   45–47, 58, 61, 63, 116, 117
Direct violence   7, 9, 29, 50, 58, 104
Disengaged citizenship   47–49, 59, 60, 63, 73, 85, 90, 116, 120
Disassociation   51, 58, 59, 73

Enemy   1, 2, 8–10, 34, 35, 40, 44–49, 51, 53, 55–59, 61–63, 67, 71, 73, 77, 85, 91, 97, 99, 117

Identity   8–10, 21, 26, 28, 33, 36, 38, 39, 45–51, 55–59, 61, 63, 64n7, 85, 88, 90, 95, 98, 102, 116, 117
International humanitarian law   24–26, 32, 83, 98, 99, 101, 106

Negative peace   2, 24–27, 59, 98, 100
Normalization of violence   1–3, 5, 7, 8, 12, 17, 25, 27n1, 29, 32–35, 37, 40, 43, 44, 49, 51–54, 57, 59, 60, 63, 65, 77, 85, 87, 90, 93–96, 104, 113, 115, 116, 120

Participatory education   78, 80, 91, 103–105

Participatory methodologies   35–38, 114
Peace epistemologies   19, 20, 87, 96–98, 106, 111
Peace work   2, 18, 20–22, 24–27, 30–33, 43, 53, 87, 89, 97, 98, 105, 109, 112–114, 116–120
Peacebuilding   1–3, 10, 20, 22–24, 26, 27, 32, 34, 36, 60, 71, 74, 76, 77, 81, 83–85, 87–107, 116, 118–120
Peacebuilding education   23, 24, 26, 34, 74, 81, 83, 84, 91, 98, 100, 116, 119, 120
Positive peace   18, 24, 26, 27, 118
Power   1–5, 10–17, 21, 22, 26, 28–42, 44, 45, 60, 63–75, 80, 81, 84, 86–88, 90–98, 102–105, 107–109, 111–117, 119, 120, 123, 124, 127

Other (Dangerous or Dehumanized)   1, 2, 8, 9, 11, 35, 49–52, 56, 57, 59, 60, 63, 70, 71, 77, 84–86, 90, 92, 95, 113, 115, 117

Relational epistemologies   19, 23, 48, 64, 86–89, 91, 92, 95, 98, 103, 106, 109–112, 114, 118–120
Respectful relations   32, 38, 77, 79, 80, 83, 84, 92, 112, 114, 120

Socialization   4, 10, 14, 15, 35, 57, 59–61, 65, 69, 90, 96, 117
Structural violence   4, 7, 93, 96
Systems of exclusion   45, 49–51, 59, 63, 71, 85, 90, 116, 120

Violence   1–12, 17, 18, 20, 21, 23–26, 27n1, 29, 31–35, 37, 40, 42–47, 49–63, 64n4, 65, 74, 76–78, 80–83, 85–99, 101, 104, 106–121
Violence transformation   2, 10, 21, 31, 76, 87–115, 118–120

Young adult   2, 3, 3n6, 10, 31–36, 39, 43n1, 44, 85–87, 104, 115, 116, 118, 121n1, 127
Youth   1–3, 3n2, n6, 4, 7, 8, 21, 28–42, 43n1, n5, 44–63, 68–87, 90–100, 103–120, 125

Printed in the United States
By Bookmasters